THE
Yorkshire Dales

THE
Yorkshire Dales

Geoffrey N. Wright

GUILD PUBLISHING LONDON

All photographs are by the author

Text and photographs
© Geoffrey N. Wright   1986

This edition published 1987 by
Book Club Associates
by arrangement with
David & Charles

Phototypeset by ABM Typographics Ltd
and printed in Great Britain
by Redwood Burn Ltd Trowbridge Wilts
for David & Charles Publishers plc
Brunel House   Newton Abbot   Devon

Published in the United States of America
by David & Charles Inc
North Pomfret   Vermont 05053   USA

CONTENTS

View across Wensleydale from above author's home at Helm, near Askrigg. The distant hill is Addlebrough

INTRODUCTION –
MY NATIONAL PARK

From the window of the room in which this is written I look out over a few square miles of Wensleydale. Southwards across the valley Addlebrough's table-top summit commands the view, its 'stepped' hillsides showing a well-loved profile so characteristic of these northern dales. To the south-east, and more distant, Pen Hill raises its massive whale-back across the horizon, and there is a glimpse of a shoulder of Little Whernside beyond. Although hidden from view, the parallel valleys of Bishopdale and Coverdale lie between. West of Addlebrough is the hollow that hides Semerwater, beyond it the distant skyline, seen so frequently from here in sombre silhouette, which marks the central watershed of the Dales, separating Wensleydale from Wharfedale and the limestone country to its south. Westwards again, Crag and Yorburgh and Wether Fell raise their friendly, unspectacular crests against the sky. It is a familiar landscape, fashioned by natural forces, shaped by eroding elements, but above all humanised by man.

The name of my house, 'Helm', has Norse origins, and apparently means 'barn'. Although the present building is mainly eighteenth century it is likely that forty or more generations have occupied this site. Like its fellows along the south-facing hillside it is on a spring line. Indeed, the outflow from a seeping well at the back runs a few feet beneath the floors in a carefully channelled course. A narrow, walled lane, still a public bridleway, passes in front of the property, cobbled beneath its covering of grass. I was told a few years ago that it was known locally as 'Lady Anne's road', probably a folk-memory from the

1670s when Lady Anne Clifford came this way during visits to her northern estates from her Skipton Castle home.

This northern side of Wensleydale above Askrigg is known as Abbotside, marking its former association with Jervaulx Abbey which for four centuries owned land here. A small community at the bottom of the hill is called Grange, where a farm has in its north wall a medieval window. It is thought that the original site of Jervaulx was here at Fors, on this spot. On the south side of the river, still within my view, its earthworks revealed in the low-angle sunlight of early morning or late evening, Bainbridge's Roman fort on Brough Hill takes the human element of my view into a remoter past. Even more conspicuous is the Roman road arrowing south-westwards up the flanks of Wether Fell on its course to Ribble Head, Ingleton and Lancaster. In that single feature man's additions to the landscape span fifteen centuries, for when, in 1751, Alexander Fothergill – who lived at Carr End above Semerwater – surveyed a route for the Richmond–Lancaster turnpike, he used the Roman road from Bainbridge, crossing the watershed to Gearstones. It proved too hazardous in winter, so in 1795 a new course took it through Hawes and up Widdale along the route now followed by a main road.

Stone walls which pattern the valley were built about the time of Waterloo. Apart from a few barns, and some cottages in Bainbridge, they are almost the newest structures in the landscape. Yet it is impossible to live here, or even to visit the Dales, without being aware of its cultural humus, of lives and landscapes mutually enriched but always tied to the changeless rhythm of the seasons. As I write, some Border Leicester rams are waiting to meet Swaledale ewes, and in a few months' time a new generation of lambs will greet the spring.

Through the repeated seasonal rhythms landscapes change. Colours are abundant, but soft, gentle and subtle, usually a harmony of greys, greens, duns and darker browns. Now, in late autumn, grass in the valley fields greens with the growth of Yorkshire fog – not a weather phenomenon but the name given to the maturing growth of meadow grass after its hay or silage crop has been taken. At higher levels, moor-grass of rough pasture pales and yellows, and in Whitfield Gill behind my house a glade of beech-trees glows with autumn gold. Berries of hawthorn and rowan are bright red accents, and where bracken has invaded the edge of pastures its russet hues will stay until the fullness of spring.

Winters are long, often with a few severe cold spells, and snow is usually expected. Not until April can one hope that the worst is past, but even then an unfriendly land and climate offer a hard welcome to the arriving lambs. Spring comes late to the Dales, and the lone ash-tree near my house will not be in leaf until early June. By then the mantle of wild flowers is at its brightest and best, especially on limestone landscapes. Grass is cut for silage, but the more traditional hay crop needs another month to ripen. In a normal season, hay-timing (hay-making) might be expected in late June, or early July, later still in the upper dales. If I were asked to show a visitor the Dales at their best I should take him to Muker, in Swaledale, as June yields to July, and walk through the hay-meadows to the river. Here, in one square mile of landscape is enshrined all the magical beauty of the Yorkshire Dales, all the ingredients in perfect proportions and perfect harmony: a village where life has followed the unchanging pattern of pastoral farming – 'tupping', foddering, lambing, clipping, hay-timing, and the twice-daily routine of milking cows – for a thousand years. Houses, farms and cottages span only the last three centuries, and the church is, unusually, of Elizabethan date. The valley of the River Swale stretches away northwards; on Kisdon, to the west, the ancient Corpse Way and the modern Pennine Way meet and cross; limestone scars etch background hills; scattered woodlands, field barns, and walls catch the eye, and the hay-meadows are a coloured tapestry. In such a view as this – and there are many similar in the Dales – vision seeks repose and is content.

I should walk with my visitor along the riverside path as far as the foot of Swinnergill. If he was keen, I'd take him on to Keld and return to Muker by the Pennine Way; if less active, a return by the river would be just as rewarding. If my friend remained unaffected by all this beauty then I'd realise the Dales were not for him, and I should be sad.

If upper Swaledale represents, for me, the quintessence of the Yorkshire Dales, my own little corner of Wensleydale, home for many years, is a fine microcosm of the natural and man-made landscapes. It is the balance and interaction between these which give the area its distinctive quality. At times intimate and appealing, at others vast and hostile, it is a landscape where geological events have juxtaposed hills and valleys into a relatively compact area, exploited yet enriched by man to a degree readily appreciated in almost any single view, certainly in any short walk.

For me and for many others walking is the best way physically to experienced landscape, to become absorbed into it, and feel its changes of mood. The senses can perceive its subtleties of sights, sounds, smells, even of touch: the difference between limestone, sandstone, and gritstone; the friendly shelter of walls; the scent of hay or wild flowers or fungi in October woodlands; the springiness of sheep's wool; cool, clear water in chuckling becks which tumble and frolic down the hillside to join the River Ure in the broad valley bottom.

Beyond the limits of my view hundreds of becks, and dozens of little valleys, each a Dale in its own right, contribute their themes to the majestic symphony of the Yorkshire Dales, but it is the names of the three major valleys which are engraved on the hearts of those who live here, and those who visit for recreation. Swaledale is sinuous, grand, tinged with the melancholy of vanished industry, and, especially above Gunnerside, has an austere beauty that tugs at the heart-strings. Above all others it is the dale for adventurous youth first to love. Wensleydale is mature, green, and full of fertile farmland. Wharfedale is sometimes mischievous and lively, sometimes reflective, always lovely, with a sylvan quality in its lower reaches which makes it specially favoured.

Ribblesdale and Malhamdale, which is really upper Airedale, embrace the wide, limestone landscapes of the Craven uplands, geologically if unmusically called karst country, where water plays strange tricks, and whose magic is as much underground as on the surface. Nevertheless, for ordinary mortals like me, the scars, crags, cliffs and pavements of limestone country are a constant delight, and often I wonder why it is that the wild flowers of the limestone seem brighter-coloured than those elsewhere.

The westwards-flowing rivers of Dee and Clough have valleys of great intimacy and charm, patterned more by hedges than by walls. They have the additional virtue of meeting near Sedbergh at the southern foot of the Howgill Fells – smooth, rounded, green hills structurally of Cumbria and now administratively within Cumbria, although their southern portion remains within the Yorkshire Dales National Park. Other dales, some not traversed by through roads, are the supporting cast in the whole theme – Arkengarthdale, Bishopdale, Colsterdale, Cotterdale, Coverdale, Crummackdale, Grisdale, Littondale and Walden. Each is an individual, different from its fellows; each has a story to tell, paths to explore, houses and farms to be seen. Green lanes, packhorse tracks, monks' trods are quiet now; in centuries past they were busy with their appropriate traffic, a network of trading routes to markets, monasteries, castles, mines, quarries and villages. Some are now the surfaced roads along which we drive, but most are lonely ways across the hills used only by walkers and occasional farmers. History's patina enriches each.

The soft green turf, long limestone scars etching hillsides, the wilderness of upland commons, the geometry of stone walls patterning thousands of fields, the farms and barns and close-clustered villages, to-

Wensleydale, looking SE to Pen Hill, from Carperby Quarry

gether ensure that this could be nowhere else in England. Only in the Yorkshire Dales are there precisely these proportions of shapes, lines, masses, textures, colours, sounds, voices, people and buildings. Changes have occurred and are occurring but there is an underlying changelessness which, in a troubled world, is a satisfying anchorage. The native Dalesman, descended from ancient stock of Celtic, Anglian, Dane, Norse or Norman forbears, is noted more for his independence than his eloquence, and is unlikely to sing the praises of the Dales, but for him and for thousands who have made the Dales their home, as well as those who seek their own delights in the area, the Yorkshire Dales are a particular sort of paradise.

*   *   *

The Yorkshire Dales was the seventh of the ten National Parks of England and Wales to be designated, one of five in the north of England. When it was designated, in 1954, its 680 square miles of predominantly Pennine landscape were shared almost equally by the

North and West Ridings of Yorkshire. Twenty years later boundary reorganisation brought significant administrative changes, and most of the National Park is now in the county of North Yorkshire – although its north-western corner, formerly within Sedbergh Rural District, was transferred to Cumbria, so this latter county claims its allegiance and rates – and the responsibility for administering National Park functions lies in a single executive committee of North Yorkshire County Council, with some Cumbrian representation. This committee of twenty-four members includes twelve county councillors from North Yorkshire, one from Cumbria, one representative from each of the three district councils of Richmondshire, Craven and South Lakeland, and eight members appointed directly by the Secretary of State for the Environment after consultation with the Countryside Commission.

The objectives of the National Park Committee can conveniently be summarised as:

1 To preserve and enhance the natural beauty of the area.
2 To promote its enjoyment by the public.
3 To have due regard to the needs of agriculture and forestry and to the social and economic interests of the area.

Generally, conservation of landscape character, natural or man-made, and of wildlife, takes priority over recreation. Promotion of public enjoyment is interpreted as providing opportunity without positively encouraging indiscriminate recreational expansion. Most visitors to the Yorkshire Dales come by car and enjoy passive sightseeing and touring by car. Many – probably an increasing number – come to enjoy walking, either on the high moors and fells or in the valleys. Cycling is popular, but the many hilly roads militate against its ever becoming the dominant recreational activity. Specialist interests such as caving, potholing and hang-gliding are enjoyed by relatively few enthusiasts, and the various water sports have their followers. Within the Park only Embsay Reservoir, near Skipton, offers reasonable yachting facilities.

Anglers will find good opportunities in the appropriate seasons for trout and grayling fishing in the various rivers and becks. Reservoirs, and the privately owned lakes of Semerwater and Malham Tarn, offer facilities, while fly-fishing is available at Kilnsey Park in Wharfedale.

About 16,000 people live within the Park area – over 1,000 fewer than in 1951, but a shade more than in 1971. Motorways and trunk roads bring the Dales within a two-hour journey for sixteen million people, and to an increasing extent people are coming to the Dales either on day trips or for longer stays. This is not a new phenomenon.

One of the earliest recorded visits was that of John Leland in about 1546 which took him into Wensleydale and Swaledale. William Camden visited Wharfedale in 1582, and George Fox founded the worldwide Christian movement of Quakerism in the northern dales around the middle of the following century. In 1698 Celia Fiennes touched the eastern margins on her epic ride through England, while in 1724 Defoe's travels brought him to Skipton and Settle, Burnsall, Richmond and Ripon, and he described the landscape north of Settle as 'nothing but high mountains which had a terrible aspect'.

Travel became easier from the middle of the eighteenth century, with the creation of the turnpike roads, and the first tourists adventured into the Dales – people with the wealth and time to make a tour, a circular journey undertaken solely for pleasure, and with a suitable means by which to travel. Pocock in 1751, Bray in 1777, John Byng in 1792 came as tourists; John Wesley from 1744 to 1788, and Arthur Young in 1771 had different motives, but all in their different ways were pioneers visiting a relatively unknown land. The later ones may have been helped by maps and road-books produced in increasing quantities. My own copies of the relevant parts of Jefferys' map of Yorkshire, drawn to a scale of 1in to the mile and published in 1771, show the roads which these travellers and tourists took, a network much thinner than, but not vastly different from, routes followed by today's visitors.

Recent surveys undertaken on a national scale show that on a summer Sunday two-fifths of the entire population of England and Wales make trips into the countryside, an activity involving up to 18 million people. In an average year 85 per cent of us visit the countryside at some stage, almost the same percentage as the proportion of our population who are urban-dwellers. It is largely an urban-based population which visits the Dales, and their attitude can probably be traced back to the Industrial Revolution when the unspoiled character of the area represented an Arcadia of beauty and health. Compared to the slums of the growing northern industrial cities it may well have been so, but the Dales, by 1800, had their industries. Most main valleys had water-powered textile mills, and the northern dales had a thriving lead-mining industry. Coal was mined on the fells or at the head of remote valleys; packhorse trains and drovers with their beasts travelled along windy upland tracks, and there was always farming.

By the end of the eighteenth century the early pioneer travellers were being succeeded by those seeking the sublime in nature, who found themselves fascinated by the caves and crags, the gills and waterfalls so abundant in the Dales. They visited Aysgarth Falls, Bolton

Priory, Gordale Scar, and above (or below) all, the limestone caves which produced such tingling thrills of horror. The writing aesthetes were followed by the gifted artists – Cotman, Dayes, Girtin, Ward and particularly Turner, who from 1808 made annual visits for many years. In the wet summer of 1816 he covered 550 miles in three weeks, mainly on horseback, partly on foot, making 450 sketches and drawings during that tour. The Wordsworth trio travelled through Wensleydale from Leyburn to Hawes, and on through Garsdale to Sedbergh, Kendal and Grasmere, in October 1802, on William and Mary's honeymoon return home from their wedding near Scarborough. A more recent writer, James Herriot, also honeymooned in Wensleydale.

Today's visitors may take a more realistic view of the Dales, but it is difficult not to admit to those Romantic symptoms which charge the elements of landscape with a far greater significance than mere reality demands. This Romantic, or sublime, view of Nature developed in early Victorian times into a desire to know more about it, with the science of geology leading, followed by botany. Now, a century and a half later, ecology and conservation are the 'in' words. Nomenclature and attitudes may change, but I still experience a thrill at seeing mountain pansies in the sweet green turf, monkey-flowers in Arkle Beck, yellow tormentil on heathy sward, bluebells beneath silver birches on a grassy bank near my home, or, best of all, bird's eye primrose in damp limestone pastures in Bardale or near Ribble Head.

Only occasionally did the early visitors make much comment about how people lived and worked in the Dales. They were more concerned with the natural, the Romantic, and, to some extent, the frightening landscape. True, Young made terse remarks about the nature of some roads, but was more concerned with the potential for improving landscapes for farming purposes. Could he revisit the area today, two centuries later, he might be impressed.

The Yorkshire Dales continue to be an area of pastoral farming, primarily concerned with producing young stock, sheep and cattle, to send down the valleys for fattening on lusher pastures, or for butchering. Dales farms serve as a reservoir from which lowland herds and flocks are regularly replenished, while dairy cattle are still kept in large numbers for milking. However, the economies of hill-farming are such that, to rear cattle and sheep in an environment often inhospitable, sometimes actively hostile, cannot possibly compete with similar activities in more favoured locations. For example, in southern

Bolton Priory, Wharfedale

England lambing occurs from early January; here, it is April. In the south the growing season lasts at least seven months; here it is less than six. Thus, farming in the Dales, as in other upland areas, remains viable only through subsidies and special grants which aim to compensate for the natural disadvantages. These subsidies come nationally and through the EEC, but the money for them is ultimately from the tax-payer. It needs to be remembered, therefore, that in this respect society is, to some extent, paying hill-farmers to continue their farming activities, recognising that were this not so, hill-farming would cease, and the upland scene would almost certainly change for the worse. The Dales landscape without its half-million sheep and 60,000 cattle would be lifeless indeed. It is significant that the National Park symbol is the head of a fine Swaledale ram.

Unless they are gathering sheep or repairing walls you are not likely to find farmers on the high fells. Nor are you likely to meet native Dales people walking much for pleasure. It is the visitors who walk and explore. The year 1864 saw the first recorded climb on a gritstone out-crop, Crookrise Crags near Embsay, by a Yorkshire climber called Cecil Slingsby. In 1887 two teachers at Giggleswick School, Canon J. R. Wynne-Edwards and D. R. Smith, made the first Three Peaks climb – Ingleborough, Whernside and Penyghent in that order. Ten years later the challenge became competitive, when four members of the newly formed Yorkshire Ramblers climbed the Three Peaks in 10½ hours. Twelve hours for the circuit came to be regarded as par, not bad going for 5,000ft (1,525m) of climbing and 25 miles of walking. I still prefer to take one hill at a time, savouring its character, relieved that Ingle-borough is not the 1,760 yards (1,610m) high which Jefferys recorded!

Below ground, Stump Cross Cavern, between Grassington and Greenhow Hill, was discovered accidentally around 1850 by lead-min-ers opening up a shaft. Ingleborough Cave had been explored as early as 1837, but it was not until 1895 that a Frenchman, E. A. Martel, made the first descent into Gaping Gill, using a rope-ladder and with a lan-tern fixed to his arm. It took 23 minutes, but he did not stay down long, with an August storm threatening, and climbed up again in 28 minutes. Now, the 340ft (104m) descent by bosun's chair, winch-controlled, takes about 20 seconds. Your stomach follows later, and the return to the surface will cost you a couple of pounds.

Although the area is described as a National Park, almost all the land within it is privately owned, even the vast areas of upland commons. The National Park Committee does own small, fragmented pieces, mainly used as carparks at its Information Centres at Grassington,

Hawes, Aysgarth, Clapham and Malham. Sedbergh also has an information centre adjoining a public carpark, while the National Park has its own 'honesty-box' carparks at Dent, Castle Bolton and Horton-in-Ribblesdale. In order to safeguard access to, or exercise control of, certain small areas of vulnerable landscape, the National Park Committee has bought parcels of land – Freeholders' Wood by Aysgarth Falls, Langcliffe Scar and Cleatop Park Wood near Settle, and Crookrise Crags above Embsay – but these are exceptions.

The National Park Department is divided between two offices: at Bainbridge, where planning and administration are based; and at Grassington, centre also for the Field Officer in charge of the six Area Wardens. These, together with the assistants who man the information centres, are the National Park staff whom the visiting public are likely to meet. Wardens, with their Field Assistants and volunteer helpers, are responsible for footpath and footbridge maintenance and repair, for the erection and upkeep of stiles, for waymarking, for practical conservation aspects such as tree-planting, and for the important liaison work in the field between farmers and landowners, the visitor, and the National Park Committee. Additionally, they visit local schools, advise visiting groups and are responsible for organising within their own areas the guided walks which form an increasingly popular, and much appreciated, programme of activities during the holiday season. Thus, in each area the National Park Warden is the person in the front line, a countryside manager promoting both conservation and recreation.

Those who are fortunate enough to live in the area, and those who seek re-creation here, will be agreed on one thing: the Yorkshire Dales are a unique part of our heritage, which must be conserved – not ossified or turned into a huge museum, but maintained as a living landscape where people live and work. In any Dales village or small town there will be locals whose names fill columns in telephone directories – Aldersons, Dinsdales, Fawcetts, Ivesons, Metcalfes, Middletons, Sedgwicks – and there will be relative newcomers who have moved into the area to retire or set up a small business. Indeed, the number of people who are self-employed, or run small family businesses like shops and garages, seems appropriately large for an area noted for the independence of its natives. Farming predominates, however, and must continue to do so, even though it is dependent on urban markets.

This illustrates one aspect of the complex, often subtle, interrelationship between town and country. Many of the shops and garages referred to benefit from the seasonal influx of visitors from nearby towns and cities; the eyesore quarries meet industrial needs; the popular Dales

Rail, which has helped to sustain the life of the famous Settle–Carlisle railway, is largely dependent on urban-dwellers from West Yorkshire and Lancashire. It is deeply to be regretted, however, that other aspects of public transport in the Dales are less satisfactory.

There is, for example, no Sunday bus service in Swaledale or most of Wensleydale, nor can you get to or from Malham by bus on a Sunday morning – a remarkable state of affairs in an important National Park.

The loss of the country bus is only one of the changes for the worse in the Dales. Before I lived permanently in the area I visited it frequently, almost annually during the 1950s, many times each year during the next decade. Thus, the changes I have noticed have been largely incremental, happening bit by bit, not very noticeable at the time, but building up to big changes. A Dalesman, exiled for thirty years and not having been back since, would be rather more surprised.

Some changes he would notice are improvements. Much property has been restored, renovated, cared for, with new windows and doors, fresh paint and sound roofs, even if many houses are not occupied throughout the year. Villages certainly look more prosperous and tidy, although some of the larger ones, as well as the market towns, have expanded. There are more carparks, very many more cars; new stiles, new footpath signs, new footbridges, and yellow or blue waymark signs, and there are considerably more visitors. Road-widening may enable one to drive faster, and probably see less; the Wensleydale railway has vanished; too many village pubs have been tarted up. Especially if the returning Dalesman was a farmer, he might note with dismay that fewer upland farms were in business, but their land has been incorporated into that of valley farms. Land Rovers and tractors have replaced horses, and the hay-sleds have vanished. Bulk milk tankers collect the milk, and the old milk-kits have found their way to museums. More stock pass through markets; some farms have utilised fields for camping and caravanning, and a local industry has grown in holiday cottages, with far less damage to the environment than the ever-enlarging quarries in Ribblesdale and Wharfedale. Afforestation darkens upland hillsides in Langstrothdale, Dentdale, Garsdale, Cotterdale and Widdale.

But the rivers remain in their green valleys, against their back-cloth of friendly yet challenging hills. Traditional values and attitudes survive, and the Dalesfolk still offer a warm, though not effusive, welcome. Those who live here, or those who come, like the swooping swallows, as summer visitors, are all part of the area. The delights are for all who can see and listen, to absorb and perceive so that each individual becomes part of the human experience of the Yorkshire Dales.

1
MAKING OF THE LANDSCAPE

Rocks are the basis of scenery, and the geological history of the York-shire Dales is, in general terms, fairly clearly displayed and reasonably simple to explain. Indeed, in a 4 mile walk from Ingleton it is possible to learn a great deal about the rocks of the Dales. The Falls Walk, as it is now called, following the valley of the River Twiss, is a geological and scenic microcosm of the whole area. It starts and finishes at the carpark (694734) to the north of the old railway viaduct, and its tourist poten-tial was recognised as long ago as 1884 when Joseph Carr, with a group of local residents, formed the Ingleton Improvement Association which, over the next thirty years, created many miles of access paths and built bridges to enable visitors to view the geological wonders of 'Ingleton Glens' ('glen' having a more romantic sound to late Victorian ears than its English equivalent). Train-loads of visitors came to Ingle-ton – an estimated 100,000 people in 1893 – and the village prospered to become one of the first tourist centres in the Dales.

The picturesque scenery may have been the attraction, but at its heart lay the rocks, exposed in a succession of localities throughout the Falls Walk to create an impressively important geological itinerary well worth the admission charge to the walk. It reveals the area's basement rocks, either as natural outcrops or as quarries, crosses three major faults, a number of dykes, and near its northern end an important example of what geologists call an unconformity – a place where sedimentary strata rest on a worn surface of other rocks of a vastly dif-ferent age.

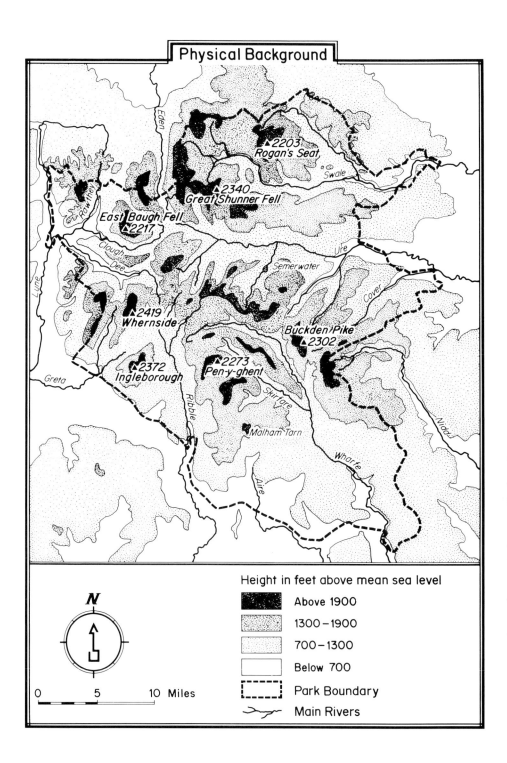

Physical Background

▲2203 Rogan's Seat

Swale

▲2340 Great Shunner Fell

East Baugh Fell ▲2217

Eden

Rawthey

Clough

Dee

Lune

Ure

Semerwater

Cover

▲2419 Whernside

Buckden Pike ▲2302

▲2372 Ingleborough

▲2273 Pen-y-ghent

Greta

Skirfare

Malham Tarn

Ribble

Nidd

Aire

Wharfe

N

Height in feet above mean sea level

Above 1900

1300–1900

700–1300

Below 700

Park Boundary

Main Rivers

0   5   10 Miles

This is at Thornton Force, where the River Twiss cascades over a notch in limestone strata into a typical 'plunge' pool. The limestone forms the upper half of the fall and overhangs the almost vertical green Ingleton slates. Between is a boulder-conglomerate forming a shallow ledge along which one can scramble behind the falling water. This ledge was once part of a beach of boulders resting on a water-worn platform beneath a sea-cliff, an exposure of rocks recognised about two centuries ago as evidence proving that past geological processes were similar to those continuing today, but spread over vast periods of time.

Thornton Force, as any other waterfall, shows the furious power of water. Although the limestone above is hard, water erodes it; the slates below are hard, but are eroded, as is the boulder-conglomerate. Back-spray, carrying rock fragments, has hollowed out at the foot of the fall an opening like an understair cupboard, so the whole fall recedes more at the base than at the top. Resulting overhangs and rock-falls provide more ammunition for erosion, so the gorge itself is also receding, even if the change is imperceptible to our eyes today.

A path continues beyond Thornton Force into Twisleton Lane and if this is followed eastwards beyond Twisleton Hall it offers a viewpoint which shows a geological section of textbook perfection. To the east is

Thornton Force, near Ingleton, showing (above) horizontally-bedded limestone; (middle) thick layer of boulder conglomerate; (below) vertical Ingleton 'slates'

Ingleborough, one of the famous 'Three Peaks', an isolated but massive mountain rising above an extensive limestone plateau whose scar edges overlook Chapel-le-Dale to the north-east. Ingleborough itself consists of limestones, shales and sandstones of the Yoredale Series of rocks, of which more will be said later. A 50ft (15m) layer of Millstone Grit forms the summit cap, while 1,500ft (460m) below, the basement rocks of the valley floor are exposed as the so-called 'Ingleton granite' – actually a massive greenish sandstone worked for roadstone – in Skirwith Quarry (705742).

Seen in the all-embracing view or appraised in close-up intimacy, the Dales landscape can be regarded as having largely originated in water, and has been shaped by water and other elements of erosion, a process remorselessly if imperceptibly continuing.

The main rocks of the area were laid down as sediments in seas, swamps and huge river deltas between 250 and 330 million years ago. Beneath them is a foundation of older rocks forming a slaty floor of a former worn-down land surface, whose undulations are the relics of ancient mountain ranges and their associated valleys formed by huge movements of the Earth's crust. These older rocks are exposed at a few places in the Craven area between Malham Tarn and Austwick, west of Ribblesdale. About one mile north-west of Helwith Bridge old workings at Arcow and Foredale Quarries, on private land, and at Dry Rigg Quarry which has a public footpath through it, show various slaty strata overlain by Great Scar Limestones, while at nearby Moughton Nab (798696) a further good example of similar unconformity can be examined more closely. Silurian slates in Crummackdale are exposed in a splendid anticline between Austwick and Crummack Farm, but the main mass of Silurian rocks is in the north-west of the National Park area where they form the smoothly rounded summits of the Howgill Fells. Barbondale, south-west of Dent, marks not only the line of the Dent Fault, but also the division between the limestones of Craven and the Silurian rocks to the west, and the Rawthey valley continues this division north of Sedbergh. Subsequent erosion and subsidence smoothed these folds, on which were deposited the Carboniferous sediments earlier mentioned. These produced the limestones and sandstones from which the Dales scenery was eventually carved.

Every part of the Dales was once beneath warm seas of clear water, shallower in the south of the area, with deep troughs in the north. Millions of tiny plants and animals lived in these warm waters, their skeletons slowly piling up as chalky mud to create the hundreds of feet of white Carboniferous limestone in which they can be recognised as fos-

Howgill Fells; smooth, rounded hills above Sedbergh, Cumbria, in the NW corner of the National Park

sils. The pure limestone of the Craven area, sometimes up to 5,000ft (1,525m) thick, known as the Great Scar Limestone, thus originated.

South of the Craven uplands is a line of prominent, though relatively small, rounded hills called reef knolls. These can be identified immediately to the east of Settle, around Malham, and south of the River Wharfe near Grassington. Their origin is uncertain, but they were probably mounds of reef debris, including coral, with lime mud, formed as heaps above the level of the sea-floor when the Great Scar Limestone was being deposited. What is unusual is that their now grass-covered slopes seem to have survived millions of years of upheaval and erosion to maintain their original profiles.

Above the Great Scar Limestone are the Yoredale Series of rocks, given this name by Philips in 1833, from their major occurrence in Wensleydale, formerly Yoredale. The Yoredales, younger in age than the Great Scar Limestone, extend to 1,000–1,200ft (305–366m) thick, their unique sequence of strata, limestone, shale and sandstone repeating itself eight times, creating the terraced scenery characteristic of Wensleydale and upper Wharfedale. A climb up the side of Wensleydale's valley at, say, West Burton, Carperby, Askrigg or Hardraw reveals the scenic effects of the Yoredales. Several times you encounter a limestone scar, then cross a gently rising shelf of good pasture, followed by a steep slope, sometimes with boulders and scree, in turn succeeded by another limestone outcrop. Above Carperby and

Burtersett the steeper slopes show quarry debris resulting from underground working of the flaggy sandstones last century. A walk from Askrigg, behind the church, leads to Mill Gill and Whitfield Gill, where water action has eroded a gorge which exposes the whole succession of Yoredale strata in almost textbook perfection. Seen in profile from any good viewpoint, the Yoredale landscape is instantly recognisable. Its limestones have weathered into long, horizontal scars outcropping to show their vertical faces to the valley. Above them the shales, being soft, have been weathered to almost flat terraces, and above these, usually hidden beneath the scree of the next limestones, are the sandstone strata which have yielded such good building stones.

The Yoredales have produced some of the best waterfalls in the Dales. Becks draining down the hillsides have created deep wooded gorges. Above Askrigg, Whitfield Beck, initially taking a level, eastward course below Whitfield Scar, turns south to cut sharply across the contours. At Whitfield Force it crashes down over the limestone and sandstone into a deep plunge pool where the force of backthrow of the water has eroded the soft shale layer. This has hollowed out an opening; the sandstone above has collapsed, bringing down the next layer of limestone, creating a waterfall of over 60ft (18m). The process has continued for thousands of years, with the resultant cutting-back of the gorge. A few hundred yards downstream the pattern is repeated at Mill Gill Force, and smaller waterfalls over thinner Yoredale sequences occur between. Farther up the dale Hardraw Force, formed over the same strata as Whitfield, is particularly impressive, with the shale-cave behind the fall big enough to allow adventurous visitors to walk and look through the curtain of water and spray. Cotter Force, above Hawes, the falls in Hawes along the course of Gayle Beck, and the delightful falls at West Burton, all illustrate the Yoredales' ability to create characteristic and intimate aspects of scenery. Within some of the cyclothems (the geological name given to one sequence of Yoredale strata), and above them, thin coal seams occur, some of which have been worked commercially.

After the formation of the Yoredales, uplift of land masses in the north of Britain created vast mountain ranges from which great rivers flowed southwards. These made enormous deltas on the sinking Yoredale seas, creating huge thicknesses of sandstones and shales of the Millstone Grit which were laid down above the Yoredale rocks. Later earth movements lifted the seabed so that more land masses were

Gordale Scar, a collapsed limestone cave, near Malham

formed, with swamps creating conditions for forests to flourish, the origin of our major northern coalfields. Again there was geological unrest, with inundations and raising of mountain chains. Great fractures occurred ('faults'), involving rock-slips with strata on one side displaced vertically by thousands of feet. In the Dales area these tend to run north-west to south-east, the Craven Fault creating the spectacular scenery of Buckhaw Brow, Giggleswick Scar, Attermire Scar, Malham Cove and Gordale Scar. Farther north the Dent Fault follows a line down the Rawthey valley, across lower Garsdale, and then along Barbondale. Probably about the same time volcanic activity to the west resulted in molten rocks being injected into parts of the existing strata, including the ores of many minerals, especially lead.

More subsidence, inundation, sedimentation and erosion by weather re-exposed and shaped the land surface we now know, with rivers maturing to create the main valleys. The area of the Dales, seen at its simplest, can be regarded as a plateau varying in height from 1,000 to 1,500ft (305–455m) above sea-level, tilted slightly from south to north and from west to east. Above this a number of gritstone-capped peaks rise to over 2,000ft (610m); below it seven main rivers and many tributaries have cut their valleys.

One major geological event completed the story – the Ice Age, which lasted about a million years and ended in about 12000BC. In Britain, the vast northern ice-sheet of Arctic origins and character extended as far south as the Thames valley and the coast of South Wales. In the Pennines it filled all the valleys and covered all the uplands to about 2,100ft (650m). Eastwards the ice was thinner, so that the foothills between the Pennines and the Vale of York were never covered.

The ice-sheet created glaciers hundreds of feet thick, moving down the valleys, scouring the landscape, smoothing the hillsides and removing all soil. V-shaped river valleys were broadened into their present, flat-bottomed U-shapes. Soft shales were eroded, leaving limestone scars even more prominent. Kilnsey Crag in Wharfedale was sharply undercut. Eroded material was carried by glaciers to a lower level, and when the ice eventually melted, this detritus was deposited as boulder-clay, thinly on the uplands, but in the valleys as lateral and transverse moraines along the sides and across the floors. These valley moraines acted as temporary dams, holding back the accumulating melt-waters which slowly deposited their own silts to form what has become rich valley land. Lateral moraines of boulder clay and gravels eventually provided well-drained sites for village settlement and dry tracks.

Many upland tarns are the result of glacial erosion, where hollows

Norber Boulders, Crummackdale. Glacial erratics of dark Silurian slate, carried by ice and dumped on a limestone plateau. The boulders are now perched on plinths of limestone

have been scoured out or small moraines have impounded streams. Malham Tarn, with its bed of impervious slates, is contained by a morainic dam (as well as an artificial one added later) at its southern edge. Above Bainbridge, Semerwater is a glacial lake similarly impounded, and at its northern edge its short-lived outflow river, the Bain, has worn a way through this morainic debris to carve a course to Bainbridge. The gorge of the River Ure at Aysgarth was formed when the melt-waters of a huge glacial lake, impounded by a gigantic morainic dam a mile thick from west to east, broke through and eroded the soft boulder-clay to the bedrock limestone.

Other scenic effects can easily be identified. Drumlins are small, oval-shaped hills of boulder-clay and pebbles deposited and shaped by moving ice, usually in a broad valley. Wensleydale above Aysgarth has at least eighty of these, the most prominent being Lady Hill, with its planted topknot of pines. A smaller one near the main road east of Worton has been slightly eroded and reveals some of its round-pebbled core. In Ribblesdale, between Ribble Head and Horton, scores of drumlins can be seen from the road or railway, and are particularly conspicuous in the low-angle sunlight of winter or in the early morning, when the oblique light reveals their 'basket-of-eggs' profile.

On Norber, a hill above Austwick on Ingleborough's southern flanks, hundreds of glacial erratics have made this a famous geological site. These boulders of dark Silurian slate were transported by ice from their original position farther up the hill, and dumped on a limestone plateau. Weathering of the limestone has lowered the level of the plateau by a foot or so, but the harder boulders have resisted, so that many of them stand now on small plinths of limestone, proud of the surrounding surface. Some pedestals show marks of the original ice scratching. The general dip of the Carboniferous rocks towards the north and east has resulted in the top of this Carboniferous Limestone forming a vast platform in the south-west of the area. These Craven uplands are the most extensive area of karst landscape in Britain, and the many square miles of bare limestone pavements are the most remarkable natural monument in the Dales. Water has made it; water has shaped it and given it a unique texture; water, wind and weather continue to carve it, keeping it pared to the bone. Water seeping into its crevices has created a unique underworld of caves and potholes, regarded with awe and horror last century, but now a place of study and exploration. Because of their porous and fractured structure and subterranean drainage, karst landscapes have few significant surface streams, and when they do occur they have a disconcerting habit of vanishing underground and appearing elsewhere as resurgences Often several streams unite underground to flow out eventually as one spring, so water-sinks are more numerous than resurgences. Tests with coloured dyes have, over a number of years, proved connections between apparently distinct streams. Probably the best-known disappearance is where the outlet stream from Malham Tarn vanishes at Water Sinks (895655), a few hundred yards south of the Tarn, near the road, and emerges as Aire Head Springs (902623), almost half a mile south of Malham village. Similarly, the water falling into the cavernous depths of Gaping Gill (751727) reappears at Clapham Beck Head near Ingleborough Cave (755711).

But it is the surface features of the Great Scar Limestone which most visitors see. If Malham Cove and Gordale Scar make Malham the obvious centre from which to appreciate the craggy delights of naked white rock, Kilnsey Crag's familiar profile in Wharfedale represents the rock's northerly bravura appearance. From a distance these huge outcrops could be mistaken for quarries. Indeed, behind Kilnsey and hidden from the roadside view, Coolscar Quarry has for some years been a source of high-purity limestone for Steetley Refractories plc, and a recent public inquiry followed an application for its extension[1].

Elsewhere in the Craven area this same pure limestone is quarried extensively, mainly to be pulverised for use as road metal. All extractive industries damage the landscape, not only visually, but also in terms of

1   A recent decision (1986) by the Secretary of State imposes an output restriction of 175,000 tonnes annually for ten years.

the movement of heavy traffic necessary to carry away their products. While it may be argued that quarrying is economically necessary, and that limestone quarries are, in the end, man-made limestone scars not vastly dissimilar to natural ones, there is an undoubted conflict with one of the main tenets of National Park policy, that of landscape conservation. Quarrying may be a true rural industry, but it inevitably consumes, rather than conserves, landscapes. And, it needs to be remembered, limestone itself is irreplaceable, except in minute quantities as stalactites and stalagmites.

Malham Cove, never a quarry, is a curved cliff of limestone, almost 300yd (274m) across and 280ft (85m) high, obviously an old waterfall that has steadily been cut back, more quickly at its lip than at the sides. Writing in 1850, Howson reported that 'twice within the last forty years the swollen waters of the Tarn have made their way over the Cove, but the torrent was dispersed in one vast cloud of spray before it reached the bottom'. Above, the dry valley called Watlowes represents the former course of Malham Water which flowed over the cliff, but which now disappears at Water Sinks.

Probably the most distinctive view of karst landscapes is the reward only of those who are prepared to walk. Two miles west of Ribblesdale, Crummackdale (which is usually reached by a lane from Austwick) is one of the 'secret' dales, with only a single farm – Crummack, near its head. To the east is the unique hill of Moughton (pronounced 'Moot'n') with its hundreds of acres of bare limestone pavement. Moughton Lane leads to Moughton Scars, and to the west, Long Lane (from Clapham) is an old pack-horse track to Selside. Moughton Scars extend for a mile between these two routes, and at their northern end, above Thieves Moss at the very head of Crummackdale, the view embraces a strange landscape, a desert of pale, pearl-grey limestone, apparently limitless although not lifeless, for a few stunted trees survive. Beyond, to the east, the lion couchant of Penyghent rears its profile. It is an arid scene of savage, natural beauty, a wilderness of bare, dry rock riven and eroded by the waters now unseen. Yet a closer exploration reveals the hidden life, the secret but luxuriant vegetation (see Chapter 7).

Karst landscapes are absent from the northern Dales. There the Great Scar Limestone has dipped sufficiently to take it below the surface, although in Wensleydale it forms part of the valley floor at Aysgarth, where its terraces have created the series of stepped waterfalls on the River Ure. In Swaledale it has vanished beneath the ground, while the Yoredales above, at a lower level than in Wensleydale, have given us the fine gorge of the Swale and the waterfall features around Keld. But much of Swaledale and its northern neighbour Arkengarthdale is Millstone Grit country. Farther north this dominates, and the moors stretch away over their dour, wind-swept, peaty miles to Stainmore and the Tees. To many this is a featureless wilderness, but to others it is the essence of north Pennine country, where individual peaks are scarce.

In the southern and western parts of the National Park the Yoredale strata and their capping of Millstone Grit have produced a number of mountain summits whose individual profiles have made them familiar friends. Ingleborough and Penyghent, Pen Hill and Addlebrough have markedly stepped profiles, although it is the massive gritstone bulk of Whernside and Great Shunner Fell that makes those mountains distinctive. The gritstone outcrops at lower levels have been utilised by man both for building materials and for recreation. In the south-east of the Park area, Barden Fell, Barden Moor and Embsay Moor have yielded good stone for buildings, and many miles of moorland tracks can be traced from abandoned quarries to villages nestling at the foot of the slopes. Simon's Seat on Barden Fell (080598) has for over a century been one of Wharfedale's most popular viewpoints, embracing the essence of Dales landscape, the geological counterpoint of gritstone and limestone humanised by farms, fields, walls and buildings.

A few miles to the west Crookrise Crags are a prominent feature seen to the east from the B6265 Skipton–Grassington road. Not only are they impressive to look at but for over a century they have provided good climbs of various degrees of difficulty. As mentioned in the Introduction, Cecil Slingsby first climbed them in 1864, in what was probably the first recorded outcrop climb in Britain, so the Crags are the probable birthplace of British outcrop climbing. Recently, the National Park Committee, anxious to safeguard access to Crookrise Crags for present and future walkers and climbers, have bought the Crags, with 25 acres (10ha) of adjoining woodland, from the Forestry Commission. Appropriately, the British Mountaineering Council have made a contribution to the cost of purchase in memory of John Midgeley, a former president of the Yorkshire Mountaineering Club.

The Millstone Grit series of grits, shales and sandstones are completely opposite in character to the limestones. Gritstone is usually coarse, pebbly and pervious to water, and – like sandstone – yields sandy, gritty, porous soils of poor fertility. Shales – laminated, soft and easily shattered – break down into heavy clays, which when mixed with sandy soils produce workable loams. But on the summit plateaux, where there is no calcium to break it down, gritstone soils accumulate organic material which impedes drainage. Soils become deficient in oxygen, lack humus and are very heavy. On the high fells and on the heather moors to the east, layers of peat, sometimes as much as 30ft (9m) thick, have accumulated. This 'blanket peat' has a unique quality, that of being a preservative, and because of this it contains a continuous record of its own development. In it are preserved not only the remains of identifiable plants but, more importantly, the pollen of trees and other vegetation which grew on and around it. Careful extraction and study of this pollen, layer by layer, are helping to piece together the story of what clothed the uplands thousands of years ago.

Some ancient peats contain pollen of the arctic plants which grew on the few higher fells that were above the ice-sheet. As the ice retreated and became confined largely to valley glaciers, the moorlands above started to develop their vegetation, first with heath, then birch scrub, followed by the growth of pine and hazel where the soils were dry. On the edge of such forests lived the first hunter-gatherers of the Mesolithic Age. Between about 8000 and 7000BC an increasingly warm climate helped this pine and hazel forest to spread, but succeeding wet conditions retarded this, with pine diminishing, peat-bogs developing and fresh woodlands forming of alder, willow, oak and elm. In these Neolithic man started to flourish, until about 3000BC.

Another climatic change to drier, warmer conditions brought lime, ash and much silver birch, and around 500BC a return to a wetter, colder climate seemed to coincide with the arrival of the Iron Age Celts who introduced to the area arable and pastoral farming. Thus, following the end of the Ice Age about ten thousand years ago, climatic changes introduced a variety of trees and plants to the Dales. Except during the warmer spells the landscape must have been similar to the frozen tundra of Siberia today. In the milder spells hippopotami, rhinoceroses and hyaenas roamed the Dales; later it was reindeer and bison. Bones of all these have been found in river gravels and caves, such as Victoria Cave near Settle.

It has taken over 300 million years for the shaping of the Dales in the landscape of today. Although the agents of geological change are constantly at work the results are so imperceptible that we can scarcely recognise them. A rock-fall, a landslip, a new deposition of river gravel, a stream undercutting at a concave bend – these are probably all we might expect to see. Against that, man's contribution, measured in time, seems insignificant, a mere ten thousand years or so, yet in terms of landscape change its effects have been enormous and it is his contribution that must next be considered.

2
FIGURES IN THE LANDSCAPE

The early humans, the hunter-gatherers, occupied various caves in the Craven limestones, and their bone tools have been discovered by the shores of Malham Tarn. Later settlers introduced tools made of flint, or of a very hard volcanic ash – from which they made crude axes and hoes – quarried on the upper slopes of the Langdale Pikes in the Lake District. With these, together with the older method of fire, clearances were made in woodland for temporary settlements and the sowing of crops. When the ground was exhausted, the settlers cleared another patch, moved and started again. From those times originated the 'henges' at Castle Dykes, Aysgarth (982873) and Yarnbury above Grassington, which were almost certainly places of communal use, whether religious or civil.

Around 3000BC a new group of settlers from the Continent started to move into Britain. A few reached the Dales and mingled with existing Neolithic dwellers. In the next millennium more followed, bringing new tools and skills. They were the builders of the great stone circles of Britain, and the hundreds of long barrows were their burial chambers. In the Dales only a few small circles survive, of which the

On the Pennine Way ascending the lower slopes of Kisdon, above Thwaite in upper Swaledale. Bracken has invaded hillsides no longer grazed by cattle. Thwaite was a Norse settlement of the early tenth century; and late last century it was the birthplace of Richard and Cherry Kearton, pioneers of wildlife photography

best is the tiny one in upper Wharfedale above Yockenthwaite (899794). Another on Ox Close (990902) above Carperby in Wensleydale, at almost 90ft (27m) across is much larger, but most of its stones have fallen and are largely obscured by grass and turf. The well-defined grassy track which passes this circle could well be one of the most ancient routes in the Dales, following well-drained land along the northern flanks of Wensleydale's natural east-west corridor.

Between 2000 and 1000BC people of the Bronze Age, entering Britain from the south and east, and later from the west, gradually mingled with the late Neolithic and 'Beaker' Folk. They introduced new tools and trades into a land where the climate was improving, and probably tramped out the early trade routes of the Dales, including that crossing Rombald's Moor, south of Ilkley. They kept cattle, grew wheat and barley, and wove cloth, and established the first significant, settled, trading, peasant communities, not only in the Dales but throughout the Pennines. One such settlement, at Dew Bottoms (912692), is characteristically situated on the limestone plateau above Cowside Beck, close to the old monks' path between Arncliffe and Malham, and can be identified by the turf boundary walls of five small fields, some incorporating huge natural boulders of limestone. Outcropping low scars of limestone are supplemented by crude walls to form simple pounds for stock, and there are visible outlines of the foundations of four circular and two rectangular huts.

A Celtic culture reached the Dales during the third century BC, mainly by a westward spread across Yorkshire from the Humber estuary. These military arrivals mingled with the existing northern tribes called the Brigantes, and established an Iron Age culture over much of the north. By AD100 their main settlements at Aldborough, Catterick and Ilkley, all on the edges of the Dales, were established. They introduced horse-breeding and continued the existing farming of the well-drained limestone soils, leaving their marks over many parts of the area, mainly as hut circles and small, irregular fields. Because many of these were on pastures that have not subsequently been enclosed, but have remained as common land, they have not been disturbed by subsequent ploughing. In low-angle sunlight or under snow cover these

The great limestone cliff of Malham Cove, 240ft (72m) high and 300yd (274m) wide, marks the site of a former waterfall, the outflow from Malham Tarn at the end of the glacial period. It is a scarp on the Mid Craven Fault which has been cut back 400yd (364m) from the original fault line by water action. Malham Beck emerges from the base of the Cove

Celtic fields can be identified by their low walls of rough stone, now turf-covered, or as gravel banks with a few large boulders. Lea Green, north of Grassington (998655) at a height of 800ft (244m), shows an impressive network covering almost 300 acres (120ha) and there is a similar survival on the western and southern slopes of Addlebrough in Wensleydale. Ingleborough's windy summit claims the only probable Iron Age fort in the Dales; a low wall 3,000ft (915m) long encloses the 15 acre (6ha) plateau where nineteen hut circles have been identified.

Thus, man was slowly but perceptibly beginning to fashion the natural landscape of the Dales. The first permanent settlements had been established after the clearance of forest cover; an early patchwork pattern of fields probably developing through a piecemeal system of enclosure represented a human addition to the palimpsest, and a sketchy system of tracks was beginning to line the valley sides and better-drained uplands. Surprisingly, the four centuries of Roman occupation of Britain which followed left very few impressions on the Dales landscape. Neither land nor climate encouraged the building of villas, although sites of these have been almost certainly identified near Middleham (135875), at Well, near Masham, and at Gargrave, west of Skipton. In the main the wild and unfriendly uplands were left to the native Brigantes who continued their Celtic way of life, although this may not always have been peaceful.

The Roman general Agricola tried to isolate and control the Brigantes by a system of forts in and at the edge of the Dales, and by roads linking these which divided the area into blocks. To the north, Stainmore Pass had forts at Greta Bridge, Bowes and Brough, while to the south, forts at Ilkley and Elslack controlled the important Aire Gap. Forts at Aldborough and Catterick were on the main route north, at the eastern edge of the Dales, while that at Low Borrow Bridge in the vulnerable Lune valley north of Sedbergh was an equivalent in the west. Almost at the centre of the Dales, the prominent drumlin of Brough Hill in Wensleydale formed an ideal site for the Roman fort of Virosidum. Overlooking the Rivers Bain and Ure, it was garrisoned almost continually from AD80 to the end of the Roman occupation, with only a brief break between AD120 and 160. Before then it had a turf rampart; afterwards this was replaced by a stone one with stone huts accommodating a cohort of 500 infantry – about the same as the present population of nearby Bainbridge. If you climb the grassy slopes of Brough Hill today, you will find little evidence on the ground of this Roman installation, although its outline is revealed in the distant view. To the south-west there is no problem in identifying the arrow-like directness

Roman Road above Bainbridge, Wensleydale. Aligned precisely on the Roman fort at Bainbridge, this section strikes south-westwards towards Wether Fell. Its course was adopted as the Richmond to Lancaster Turnpike in 1751

of the Roman road running up the hillside. This linked the fort with the important base at Lancaster, and can be followed as far as Ingleton. Initially a metalled road it becomes a walled lane straight up to Wether Fell where it reaches 1,920ft (585m). Continuing as a metalled road on Oughtershaw Side above Cam, for 2½ miles it has been incorporated into the Pennine Way before descending on a more westerly alignment to Gayle Beck. The Roman route then follows the line of the present motor road south-westwards to Chapel-le-Dale and keeps to the western side of the valley of the River Greta, roughly along the line of a minor road to Ingleton. Beyond there its course to Lancaster lies outside the National Park boundary.

Another road from the fort at Bainbridge has been traced southwards, crossing the watershed into Wharfedale, and following this valley to the important fort at Ilkley, although most of its Wharfedale course is sketchy and uncertain. Its most impressive section is from above the hamlet of Stalling Busk (919861), over the Stake to the top of Kidstones Pass, where a short section of modern road is significantly called 'Causeway', then descending by Buckden Rakes to the lower part of the carpark at Buckden. On Stake Moss itself (934825) the route is identified first as a walled lane and then as an open road following the only firm limestone ground amongst peat moor and moss. At Kidstones

Causeway it follows the modern road for half a mile before branching off as a field path, where its very straight alignment is easily identified across Buckden Rakes. At the top corner of Rakes Wood (940782) the Roman road turns south-east to descend as a limestone terrace to the foot of the wood just above the village.

Other Roman roads on the fringe of the area or completely outside the National Park include the important one from Ilkley to Aldborough, and another from Ilkley to Elslack, a few miles west of Skipton. On the western flanks of the Howgills, a narrow metalled road known as Howgill Lane runs northwards from Sedbergh, following the line of a known Roman route from Overburrow, near Burton-in-Lonsdale, to the fort at Low Borrow Bridge in the Lune gorge. For 5 miles it is within the Park boundary and in addition to giving spectacular views over the valley it provides access points for exploring the steep-sided valleys and rounded summits of the western Howgills.

The end of the Roman occupation did not bring a sudden depopulation of the Dales. The inhabitants, called for convenience Romano-British, continued to occupy and work settled, favoured sites, probably in river valleys, and it may well be that such sites attracted the next wave of settlers from the seventh century onwards. Angles, probably from northern Germany and southern Denmark, having already established footholds in eastern Yorkshire in the late sixth century, gradually moved westwards to penetrate into the lower dales by the middle of the seventh century. Generally they followed river valleys, rarely moving above the 700ft (214m) contour, although Bordley, above Grassington, is an exception at 1,150ft (350m). In contrast to the short, stocky native people the newcomers were tall, strong and fair-complexioned, and brought with them new skills in arable farming and forest clearance, for which they relied greatly on oxen, a form of animal power which was to remain in use for several centuries.

Anglian settlers also brought a new language, and place names provide clues to their new communal settlements, which were the first villages of the Dales and had names which are still familiar to the modern Dales-dweller. The suffix 'ley', originally 'leah', meaning 'a village occupying woodland clearing', not only reveals the settlement pattern but also indicates where the forests were. Wensley, Healey, Ripley, Stainley, Winksley, Grantley, Bradley, Pateley, Bewerley, Otley and Ilkley, all on the eastern edge, suggest that southwards from Wensleydale was the favoured area. Swaledale and the western valleys were clearly unsuited to Anglian arable farming. It seems that gritstone country with native oak-woods offered the best conditions for settlement and the building of crude huts for peasant farmers. Being good arable farmers, the Angles recognised land as a vital resource. They would regard woodland as similarly valuable and, knowing the need for a regular supply of timber, they almost certainly planted trees for future use – as, no doubt, did earlier dwellers in the Dales.

Later immigrants seemed to prefer more open land, above valley flood levels, and in seeking it made further penetration westwards. Many of their sites have the '-ton' element in their names, as in Brompton, Burton, Witton, Carlton, Worton, Grassington, Bolton, Horton, Ingleton and Skipton. These may have been smaller homestead settlements of pioneering families practising a simple pastoral farming based on sheep, only cultivating sufficient arable land to meet their needs. In time these smaller places developed into communities, so by the eighth century the present village pattern of the Dales had already been marked out, although it was by no means complete.

After a century of relative peace Danish raids on the East Coast introduced a period of turmoil, and from about 870 the Danish conquest of Northumbria and the subsequent peace allowed Danish settlers gradually to move into the Dales, generally staying in the lower valleys and preferring to seek unoccupied land for their settlements. The '-by' place name element may indicate an original Danish settlement or the renaming of an existing Anglian village occupied by the Danes. Later Danish sites may be represented by '-thorpe', often a secondary settlement in the outlying part of an Anglian village, as in Agglethorpe-with-Coverham in Wensleydale and Burnsall-with-Thorpe in Wharfedale. In Swaledale Danish penetration only reached Easby, while in Wensleydale the limits were at Carperby and Thoralby. The name 'Kirkby', meaning a village with a church, usually associated with a personal or location name, as at Kirkby Malham, Kirkby Lonsdale and Kirkby Stephen, probably represents Danish field-church villages, and hints at a more peaceful type of penetration.

Early in the tenth century came the last major settlement into the Dales, another predominantly peaceful infiltration, this time from the west. The new wave of colonisers, moving round the coasts of northern and western Scotland, had established footholds there, as well as in Ireland and on the Isle of Man, and eventually on the north-western coast of England, from where they penetrated into the valleys of Lakeland. From west of the Pennines it was easy for them to seek new, unoccupied lands, preferring remote valley heads of Ribblesdale, Dentdale and Garsdale and then crossing the main watershed into Arkengarthdale, Swaledale, Wensleydale and Wharfedale. Favouring a pastoral system

Limestone pavements at Malham, with old and new fields beyond; Iron-Age fields near centre and medieval lynchets to right, with late-eighteenth-century enclosures superimposed

of farming based on sheep, they found the Pennine uplands very suitable and established farms apart from each other, in marked contrast to the close-knit villages of Anglian and Danish settlement. Thus the new immigrants did not compete for land with the existing communities but, in terms of land use, complemented them. Mingling and intermarriage among the successive waves of 'incomers', to use a modern word, has brought down into successive generations the colours and characteristics which today's Dalesmen have inherited. Independence, self-sufficiency and a willingness to help one's neighbour are some of these characteristics, allied to a love of the land and its stock which, if never expressed, is almost always implied.

One aspect of the Norse way of life, which involved farmers and shepherds spending much of their time on the uplands, is the evocative series of words, found in the western Dales and in the Lake District, for natural features of the landscape. Adding their own music to the moorland map are 'fell', 'rigg', 'clint', 'crag', 'scar', 'beck', 'gill', 'mere', 'moss' and 'tarn'. Place names illustrate the pattern of settlement. 'Thwaite', meaning either 'a clearing' or 'a field sloping down to a valley', is the name of a Swaledale village, and also occurs as a suffix in Langthwaite, Yockenthwaite, Swinithwaite, Hebblethwaite and Hampsthwaite.

Norse farming needed summer pastures on the fells, winter ones in the higher parts of the valleys. A Norse farmer's house was a *saetr*, either by his summer or winter pastures. This element now occurs as '-satter', '-seat', '-sett' and '-side', and examples of these are common in the Norse-settled areas. Within a few miles of Hawes, the names Appersett, Burtersett, Countersett and Marsett indicate Norse roots, while Barden Scale, Scale Park, Southerscales and Winterscales, deriving from the element *skali* were temporary shelters used by Norse shepherds and farmers.

A few examples of Norse or early medieval 'long-houses' have been located and surveyed by Dr Raistrick, almost all on rough limestone pasture at about the 1,000ft (305m) level. Stone foundations 30ft (9m) long and up to 15ft (4.5m) wide, with a central partition, suggest that half was used for living in, half for sheltering stock when necessary. Such structures were usually solitary, rarely in a group of more than three, and it is particularly significant that this shape and size is virtually identical to the two-bay houses and barns seen throughout the Dales today. Looking at the isolated farms in the upper Dales, in Ribblesdale and in the western Dales, one can identify a settlement pattern scarcely changed for a thousand years. Names of present-day farms in these areas of Norse settlement suggest a remarkable continuity of site occupation: Eskeleth, Thursgill, Helm, Birk Rigg, Knudmaning, Keld Gill and Flust. These are more than mere map names. A journey up Swaledale beyond Reeth shows in almost every view the dispersed hill farms, a pattern even more pronounced in the upper valley from Gunnerside to Keld. If the moorland road is taken to Tan Hill, with a return to Reeth by way of Arkengarthdale, the northern side of the valley between Whaw and Langthwaite is as good an example of Norse settlement as anywhere in the Dales.

Anglian and Danish villages were, by contrast, close-knit units occupied by a few families whose homes and farmsteads were probably carefully related to the natural features of a chosen site, avoiding damp places, but positioned near to a stream or spring. In the Dales, as throughout much of the country, there is no typical village lay-out, although it is apparent that a number of villages of Saxon origin may have had buildings grouped round a central open space – now the green; Reeth, Redmire, East Witton, West Burton, Arncliffe and Linton are the best-known examples. There is no evidence to support the theory that village greens like these, surrounded by houses of the village, were created as livestock refuges. Indeed, such open spaces remain something of a mystery. However, when inhabited in pre-Conquest times these settlements would have resembled African villages of thatched wooden huts rather than the apparently timeless places we see today.

The legacy of almost five centuries of successive infiltrations of the Dales, superimposed upon and gradually integrated with a native Romano-British or Celtic population, is seen in the sites of villages and farms, the naming of features of the natural landscape including rivers and hills, the slow evolving of inter-village tracks, and the characteristics of the people themselves. No buildings, other than a few stone crosses, survive from those pre-Conquest years. Easby church, near Richmond, has a plaster cast of an eighth-century cross, the original being in the British Museum. Burnsall church has fragments of tenth-century crosses, while Wensley has two small, carved grave slabs of about the same date. At Aysgarth an Anglian tenth-century cross-head was probably part of a sepulchral cross, not a preaching one, suggesting that here there was an active parish with church and churchyard at that time. It is known that pre-Conquest churches existed also at Conistone, Giggleswick and Kirkby Malham, although nothing of that period survives in the masonry. For the people who worshipped in them, and their successors through medieval times, life would have been hard, almost a battle for survival, yet relatively secure in small villages and hamlets. Nevertheless, we need to be wary about judging medieval life according to our own standards and experience.

3
THE MEDIEVAL LANDSCAPE

At the time of the Domesday survey of 1086 the population of the Dales was probably about three thousand – little more than that of either Settle or Sedbergh today and less than that of Richmond. Shortly after the Conquest, and following a northern rebellion, Duke William's 'Harrying of the North' devastated much of central Yorkshire, reaching up into the eastern margins of the Dales. It is not surprising that Domesday recorded so much of the area as *Wasta est* – 'It is a waste'. Even then, this did not cover the upper valleys, for there is no reference to Swaledale above Reeth, Wensleydale above Askrigg, Wharfedale above Hubberholme, and Ribblesdale above Stainforth. Beyond lay forest set aside for hunting, although existing Norse-settled farms were allowed to continue as Norman-controlled 'vaccaries', where keepers grazed cattle in small fenced areas, and looked after the deer.

Castles

The new Norman aristocracy hunted in the 'forests' – areas of waste land which were not necessarily woodland. The Lords of Richmond used Swaledale, Arkengarthdale and the 'New Forest'; those of Middleham hunted Wensleydale south of the river and Bishopdale, and the Lords of Skipton exploited Littondale and Langstrothdale Forest. The Norman lords lived in castles, the first permanent buildings, as well as the largest, to appear in the Dales. Each started as a small wooden structure, soon to be replaced by the massive stone for-

Middleham Castle, from the south. The twelfth-century keep rises above the surrounding thirteenth-century walls, which have angle-towers

tresses whose ruins we so much admire today. Count Alan Rufus, cousin of William, started to build the castle at Richmond in 1071, and the ground floor of the keep, formerly the gatehouse, dates from then, together with Scolland's Hall and the east curtain wall. The keep itself was added a century later, in 1170–4, while other additions and changes were made up to the fourteenth century. But in its massive display of might, Richmond Castle is distinctly Norman and was large enough to house a small army of officials, servants and military followers.

What can be seen at Middleham is a huge keep of the 1170s, with a later curtain wall with angle towers surrounding it at a distance, and a chapel added to the keep in the late thirteenth century. During the fourteenth and fifteenth centuries, domestic and living quarters were built inside the curtain walls on three sides, resulting in a very cramped courtyard. By then the castle and Honour of Middleham had passed through marriage to the Nevilles of Raby, and in 1471 – after the death of Richard Neville, Earl of Warwick, in the Wars of the Roses – it became Crown property. Ten years earlier the young Duke of Gloucester, later Richard III, joined the Middleham household for tutorage and training under the Nevilles, subsequently courting and marrying Anne Neville with whom he made a home there from 1472 to 1483. Their only son, Edward, is supposed to have been born in the south-west corner tower in 1473.

The principle of having living quarters round a central courtyard may well have been copied from the arrangement at Bolton Castle, a few miles up Wensleydale on the valley's northern flanks. By far the most important castle within the National Park area, Bolton represents 'a climax of English military architecture' (to quote Pevsner), a balance between the needs of defence and the claims of comfort, with the latter more favoured. Built by Lord Scrope from c1378 it had four massive corner towers with domestic ranges between. Except for the north-east tower, which collapsed in 1761, it survives almost complete to its full height, with no later external changes except for seventeenth-century windows in the west range. Seen from the southern approach up the hill it looks formidably powerful.

Skipton, however, seems almost welcoming, but only a gateway, in Conduit Court, survives of Robert de Romille's Norman structure. Much of what is to be seen is fourteenth-, sixteenth- and seventeenth-century building. Like Richmond Castle, those at Middleham and Skipton housed a host of retainers and followers. Towns evolved to serve the needs of Norman lords and their castle garrisons, as well as to enjoy the protection of such buildings, and their resulting trading potential was soon recognised by the granting of market charters. Thus, the three Norman castle-towns of the Dales – Richmond, Middleham and Skipton – each lying just outside the National Park, became focal points for early trading routes to their markets. Each today is at an important point of entry to the Dales, although only Richmond and Skipton retain market importance. Through medieval times, however, the social importance of the castle-towns and their markets must not be overlooked, for they probably initiated a slow expansion of peasant horizons from village to town, creating an awareness of the wider world at the edge of the Dales. In this, another foreign overlordship was soon to play its part.

Monasteries

Nine centuries have passed since Domesday, and for four of those the monasteries exerted a powerful influence – probably more benign and far-reaching than that of the castles – on lives and landscapes. Most founders of monasteries came from France, and it was the White Monks of the Cistercian Order who first settled in the Dales, having been granted land by one or other of the Norman lords. Fountains Abbey was founded in 1132; and Jervaulx initially at Fors near Askrigg in 1145, but moved to a new site in 1156. Augustinian canons settled at Bolton, in Wharfedale, in 1155, and other foundations were established at Coverham in 1202 and Easby in 1152, while small nunneries were founded in Swaledale, at Marrick in 1156, and at Ellerton near by about seventy years later. Monasteries beyond the Dales also played a significant part through owning large estates there – Bridlington, Byland, Furness and Sawley. Between them, Fountains, Furness, Sawley and Byland were granted most of the rich limestone country between Wharfedale and Ribblesdale; Jervaulx owned that part of Wensleydale on the north side above Askrigg, now the civil parish significantly called Abbotside; Byland and Fountains shared Nidderdale; Bridlington had much of Swaledale; and Bolton Priory's land was in upper Airedale. Thus through medieval times the Norman lords and the monasteries between them owned almost all the land which is now within the National Park.

The huge estates granted to the monasteries were ideal country for sheep-runs. They also included mineral resources of coal and lead-ore both of which were exploited. But it was the sheep-farming of the upland pastures which yielded so much monastic wealth and laid foundations for various aspects of life in the Dales which was to follow.

Monastic estates were managed from 'granges' – dual-purpose buildings combining hall, refectory, chapel and working farm. A priest-monk would be in charge and say Mass. Lay brothers and local people would carry out the day-to-day farming tasks. From the parent abbey or priory the 'cellarer' would make regular visits to check stores and accounts, and hold occasional courts. Sometimes he would have been accompanied by the abbot or prior who would always travel in style with servants and even bodyguards. Generations of local peasants would watch these processional comings and goings just as they would have witnessed the hunting expeditions of feudal Norman lords. Such journeys by monastic or military authorities would have quickly brought about a developing network of roads and tracks, routes also taken by pack-horse trains carrying stores, as well as by movement of stock on the hoof. Mastiles Lane, now a splendid green road for walkers and cyclists, is the most famous of such monastic tracks, linking the

Jervaulx Abbey; the dormitory wall, c1200

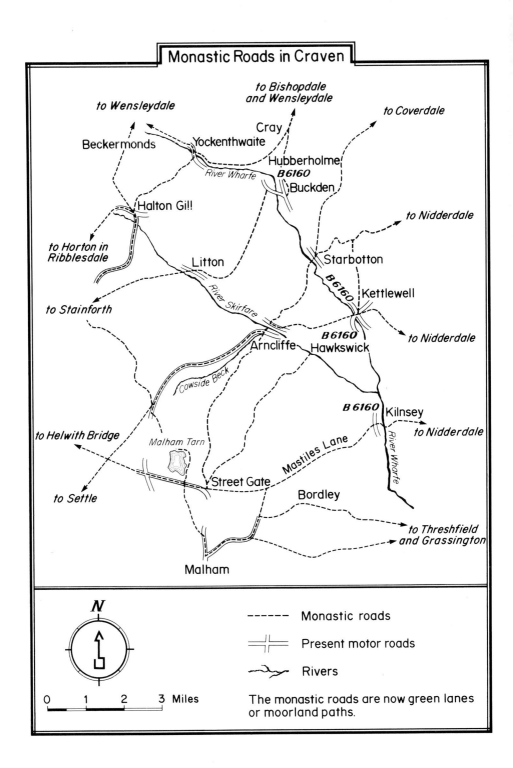

Monastic Roads in Craven

to Wensleydale

to Bishopdale and Wensleydale

to Coverdale

Cray

Beckermonds

Yockenthwaite

Hubberholme

B 6160

Buckden

River Wharfe

Halton Gill

to Nidderdale

to Horton in Ribblesdale

Litton

Starbotton

B 6160

Kettlewell

to Stainforth

River Skirfare

Arncliffe

Hawkswick

B 6160

to Nidderdale

Cowside Beck

to Helwith Bridge

Malham Tarn

B 6160 Kilnsey

River Wharfe

to Nidderdale

Mastiles Lane

to Settle

Street Gate

Bordley

to Threshfield and Grassington

Malham

N

0   1   2   3 Miles

- - - - - Monastic roads

+ + + Present motor roads

Rivers

The monastic roads are now green lanes or moorland paths.

Mastiles Lane, looking east; a famous monastic track linking the Malham Moor estates of Fountains Abbey to the important grange at Kilnsey

Malham estates of Fountains Abbey with the important grange at Kilnsey (973628). From there its course went to Conistone and then either through Grassington and Pateley Bridge or by Scot Gate and Sandy Gate to Middlesmoor, Ramsgill and Dallowgill. To the west its course is traceable, mainly as walled lanes or roads, identified now as Henside Lane and Moorhead Lane, before crossing the River Ribble at Helwith Bridge, and continuing past Wharfe and Austwick to Clapham, through Newby Cote to Ingleton, then north-westwards towards the Lake District where Fountains owned lands in Borrowdale.

Newby was a grange of Furness Abbey, and Newby Hall (728700) is a pre-Reformation house whose fifteenth-century windows in its gables may be those of the former chapel of the grange. A single window of similar date or earlier, now blocked up, can be seen (from a public foot-path) on the north wall of Chantry Farm at Grange (935908) west of Askrigg, which was Jervaulx Abbey property, while at Kilnsey Old Hall (973678) in Wharfedale a small outbuilding at the entrance to the courtyard is all that survives of the fifteenth-century gate-house of Kilnsey Grange.

At both Jervaulx and Easby very little of the monastic churches survive, and the main interest, apart from their beautiful settings – Jervaulx in private parkland near East Witton, and Easby by the River Swale just outside Richmond – is in the architecture of the domestic

Kilnsey Old Hall, Wharfedale, where Lady Anne Clifford occasionally stayed overnight on her journeys. It was built in 1648 on the site of a former monastic grange

quarters. Jervaulx's great glory is the ruined dormitory with its range of beautiful lancet windows of c1200. Easby, whose Premonstratension canons followed similar principles to those of the Cistercian monks at Jervaulx, has an unorthodox lay-out, probably the most unusual in England. There is a fine fourteenth-century gate-house but it is the noble refectory (c1300), in the south range and standing to almost full height, which commands the scene.

Coverham Abbey, in private grounds by the River Cover south-west of Middleham, has meagre remains. Approached through the ruined arch of a small gate-house (c1500), they can be seen from a public bridle-way. Three piers and two arches of the south arcade of the abbey church (1340), stand in a garden, while the early-sixteenth-century guest-house was incorporated into a seventeenth-century house after the Dissolution. Its low, nine-light window is probably the most handsome window in a private house in the Dales! Swaledale's two small nunneries, at Marrick and Ellerton, have very scanty remains. Apart

Wharfedale, below Burnsall, looking towards Appletreewick, showing the smooth valley floor with late-eighteenth-century enclosure walling. Above is broad-leaved woodland, then open gritstone moor

from the tower, Marrick's priory church was pulled down and rebuilt in 1811. Some priory buildings were incorporated into a later farmhouse adjoining on the south. Ellerton Priory, only a ruined tower, mainly fifteenth century, stands forlornly in a field by the river.

It is Bolton Priory's haunting beauty and the serenity of its riverside setting amid the wooded parklands of lower Wharfedale which make it so memorable, so admired. Alice Romilly gave Bolton to Augustinian canons who moved there from nearby Embsay in 1152, and it is the church, rather than the domestic quarters of the priory, which survives, part in ruins and part in use as a parish church. Indeed, the nave always was parochial. Although the church was started in about 1170, it was not finished until the middle of the thirteenth century. The chancel, now ruined, was extended from 1325, and the west tower, begun under Prior Moon in 1520, was never completed, work being halted at the Dissolution. Sufficient had already been built, however, to obscure the ornate, mid-thirteenth-century west front of the nave. Within the last few years, the unfinished tower has been roofed over with laminated timbers and its windows have been glazed. The floor area beneath is a reception area for the thousands who visit this glorious building, following in the artistic footprints, as it were, of Turner, Girtin and Ruskin, and countless other artists inspired by the beauty of what is virtually a man-made landscape.

Monasteries may have started out with unworldly ideals, but these did not prevent their trading to an increasing extent. It was not long before their austere way of life gave way to better standards of living, especially in the houses of abbots and priors, whose life styles came to resemble those of local lords of the manor. Monastic incomes came mainly from the annual wool crop, and to a lesser extent from trade in mineral wealth. Under monastic rule hundreds of acres of rough scrubland were cleared, and many marshy areas of valleys drained, to gain more pasture. On their farms and granges land management and sheep-breeding skills were introduced, laying the foundations of some hill-farming practices of today. It is probable that under their monastic landowners some of the old Norse farms revived their skills in breeding

Old Gang lead-smelting complex, Swaledale. In the Hard Level Gill, between Swaledale and Arkengarthdale, this is one of the best known groups of buildings associated with lead mining and smelting. Lead was worked here from the late seventeenth century. The buildings, dating from c1770–1810, include the remains of smelt-mills, flues, a roasting furnace, blacksmiths' shop, a store, and – on the skyline – the remarkable peat store livestock. Monastic records show that as early as the thirteenth century it was becoming increasingly common practice on their estates to enclose small fields by stone walls, mainly in order to keep other animals off their land. How effective these were against preying wolves is not known, but an early fourteenth-century Account Roll of Bolton Priory lists regular payment to 'the wolf-slayers'. Some early walls survive – or, at least, there are still walls in the same position, even if their appearance has changed. Above Malham, on the slopes of Cawden (904634), a small group of enclosures called Raikes Paddocks may be the walled fields named in a thirteenth-century agreement between Fountains Abbey and Bolton Priory.

Churches

Churches in the Dales are not so 'typecast' as those of, say, Somerset, East Anglia or the Cotswolds. The area was much poorer, and in the remote hill country of the upper dales parishes were large in area, with scattered hamlets sharing one central church. Aysgarth parish covered over 80,000 acres (32,000ha) of Wensleydale, while Grinton's responsibility in Swaledale could not have been much less. Many villages had and still have no Anglican church. West Burton and Thoralby used that at Aysgarth, as did Bainbridge and Askrigg until a chapel of ease was built at Askrigg in the fifteenth century. In Wharfedale, villagers of Grassington, Hebden and Threshfield continue to use their ancient parish church near Linton, situated so as to be convenient for all four townships. Dentdale was served by the parish church in Dent, Ribblesdale by that at Horton, and Littondale by Arncliffe church.

Although parishes were well established by the time of the Conquest, and many small churches were built during the eleventh and twelfth centuries, only a few Norman fragments survive – at Grinton, Redmire, West Witton, Linton, Conistone, Hubberholme, Horton and Dent. If a regional style is to be identified it is likely to be the Perpendicular style of the fifteenth century, in churches of long, low profile, a west tower, and an interior arrangement that shows no division between nave and chancel. Grinton, Dent, Askrigg, Kirkby Malham and Giggleswick are characteristic examples, the first two also illustrating how beautifully the churches sit into the landscape. However, nineteenth-century restoration or complete rebuilding yielded its usual crop of undistinguished buildings, so the church-amateur in the Dales needs to be selective. Some are worth singling out and my list would certainly include the following.

Wensley has the finest church in the National Park, mainly of the thirteenth to fifteenth centuries, and largely the result of the patronage of the powerful Scropes of nearby Bolton Castle. Early benches, box pews, a medieval reliquary, a screen which came from Easby Abbey, and the seventeenth-century Scrope family pew, make for an interior of outstanding interest, while the outside view, either from the river bridge or Wensley's small village green, is memorable. A few miles up the valley, Aysgarth's church, in its 4 acre (1.6ha) churchyard, although a rebuilding of 1866, contains two fifteenth-century screens and reading-desk, all of which came from Jervaulx Abbey at the Dissolution of the Monasteries. The larger screen is the most outstanding piece of Cistercian woodwork in North Yorkshire and may well have been constructed by the famous medieval school of Ripon carvers.

Wharfedale has two gems of churches. Reached by field paths, one of which crosses the river by stepping-stones, or along a 'no through road', St Michael's at Linton, near Grassington, is largely a fourteenth-century rebuilding of an earlier structure, its quirky profile enhanced by a short, square bell-turret with a pyramid roof. Inside is a pre-Reformation stone altar and a Jacobean pulpit, and the furnishings include a Romanesque Crucifixus carved in brass.

In upper Wharfedale, St. Michael's, Hubberholme, is for thousands of visitors the quintessential Dales church. Serenely situated by the river, its squat profile, echoing the limestone landscape beyond, hides an interior rough but not crude, homely without being quaint. Its 1558 rood loft is a rarity, one of only two in Yorkshire, brightly painted in red, gold and black. Almost all the other woodwork is modern, high-quality English oak from Robert Thompson's famous Kilburn workshop near Thirsk. One of the great delights in Hubberholme is to seek his trade-mark carved mouse tucked in out-of-the-way corners. A modern window in the south wall displays in charming detail a visual summary of parish history. If one can be said to love a church as a building, this must be a prime candidate.

For setting as well as interest, the churches at Muker and Dent are supreme. St Mary's at Muker is that rarity, an Elizabethan church. It was built as a chapel of ease to the mother-church at Grinton, in 1580, but regrettably Victorianised so that the original is obscured. The date 1714 on the south door may represent the building of the tower. Seen from across Muker Beck, and occupying almost the highest point in the grey stone village, the church is also at the focal point of the lines of hills forming a noble background. St Andrew's at Dent shares this scenic asset, but is altogether bigger and grander, proud above the stone-flagged roofs and whitewashed houses of the village. Most of the woodwork is seventeenth century, and the chancel floor is uniquely made of local Dent marble, bordered with a limestone marble from Barrow-in-Furness.

To a population living in crude wooden huts or hovels, probably heather-thatched, these churches, with their bright colours of glass and paint, their carvings in stone and wood, must have seemed to represent a different world from that of life's daily toil. Ritual and services in dialect-flavoured Latin would not have been understood, but there would have been occasions, only too rare, of sharing in local rejoicing, at the great church festivals, probably at Rogation and harvest. Churchyards were places not only for burial, but for trade, sometimes a market. For every activity, the church was the focal point.

Fortified houses

During medieval times, Dales people continued to experience danger, from a hostile climate, a harsh overlord, or even from Scots across the Border. From about 1300 to the Union of Crowns in 1603, the northern counties of England suffered from the constant threat of Scottish raids. Medieval lords enjoyed the protection of their castles and lesser gentry built fortified houses, a few of which still survive in the Dales.

Nappa Hall near Askrigg, its towers glimpsed through the trees below the northern road in Wensleydale, is justly famous. Built by Thomas Metcalfe in about 1460, its exterior is remarkably unchanged, although the four-storey west tower is little more than a roofed shell, as is the single-storey hall adjoining on the east. The lower east tower is a slightly later addition, and the south wing, now part of a working farm, was added in the seventeenth century. A good view of Nappa Hall is obtained from the public footpath which passes its western side and leads to Nappa House by the river.

Barden Tower in mid-Wharfedale, now ruined, is said to have been built by Henry Clifford, the 'Shepherd Lord', in the late fifteenth century, although it was probably more accurately an enlargement of an existing hunting lodge of the Cliffords. The chapel and priest's house were added at that time, but when the redoubtable Lady Anne Clifford inherited the family estates about 1657, she set about a vast programme of restoration. As a result, her changes to Barden have left a confusing

Nappa Hall, a fortified towerhouse c1460, near Askrigg, Wensleydale

structure in which it is hard to distinguish between fifteenth- and seventeenth-century work.

Hellifield Peel, a mile outside the National Park boundary south of Settle, is also a roofless ruin. Dating from 1440 it was a large, complex tower-house remodelled in the seventeenth century and again in Georgian times, but it still retains medieval features. Also just outside the Park boundary on the north is Walburn Hall between Richmond and Leyburn, a fifteenth- and sixteenth-century fortified house. Largely hiding behind its battlemented south wall, it was built round a courtyard, and is now a working farm. The big detached chimney seen from the road to the east may have been part of the brew-house.

In the austerely beautiful valley of Mallerstang, threaded by the Hawes–Kirkby Stephen road, Pendragon Castle represents another Lady Anne Clifford restoration. Originating as a timber tower in late Norman times it had a troubled history and had been ruinous for a century before Lady Anne began work in 1660, but was largely dismantled again twenty-five years later. However, recent patient, private clearance and excavation by its present owner, Mr Raven Frankland, has revealed more of its structure. Formerly of three storeys, it is over 60ft (18m) square with thick stone walls and corner buttresses.

Land use and villages

Tower-houses, castles, churches and monastic buildings, all constructed of stone, are the only pre-Reformation structures in the Dales. Of the houses lived in by the majority of the people we know nothing and can only surmise. We know very little more about the landscape itself, although some features seen today can be attributed to medieval land use.

In Wensleydale below Aysgarth, in Wharfedale below Grassington, and around Malham, relics of medieval farming are clearly seen in the landscape, especially in low-angle sunlight or under a light cover of snow. The corrugated or corduroy pattern of ridge-and-furrow belongs to the centuries after the Saxon and Danish settlement; strip lynchets introduce their staircase pattern on many hillsides, a legacy of land-hunger probably in the thirteenth and fourteenth centuries. Each needs a brief explanation.

Beyond their immediate ring of crudely walled crofts, Anglian villages had their common fields – ploughlands divided into strips by householders. Beyond these again were the common pastures, with woods and poorer quality land, extending up the hillsides to the moorland 'wastes'. The individual's unit of land was not so much the strip but the actual plough ridge, itself not the creation of single operation, but the consequence of several seasons' ploughing by a heavy medieval plough capable of completely turning over a sod. Ridge-and-furrow is formed by first ploughing a furrow in one direction, say north to south; the resultant sods are tipped over to the right, that is, the west; on the return run, cutting a parallel furrow, sods are turned inwards, that is, to the east, to lie against the first ones. Third, fifth, and subsequent north–south runs each tip their sods over the first, while 'even' numbered runs tip theirs against the second row, and so on. Thus, when a plough ridge is completely ploughed, all the strips of sods are tilted inwards. In time, these would build up into the raised ridge we see today, with consequent broad furrows between the ridges. There is a remarkable consistency in the lateral distance between these, usually 15–20ft (4.5–6m). An individual's strip of land would usually have consisted of between two and five adjacent ridges, roughly a furrow (furlong) long, and the series of peasant strips were grouped together in one open field, without walls or hedges. An Anglian village would probably have had two or three such fields, and its seems probable that any crop rotation would have been practised on individual furlongs rather than whole fields.

Strip lynchets are easy to recognise, and splendid examples occur between Carperby and Castle Bolton in Wensleydale, in Littondale, near Conistone in Wharfedale, on both sides of the valley between Grassington and Burnsall, and around Malham. They are particularly prominent in the view from the road when travelling from Kirkby Malham to Malham. Significantly they are absent from the western Dales and any areas of Norse settlement. They are usually, but not always, found on steep hillsides above the normal levels of ploughed fields, and represent the exploitation of hitherto unploughed land by medieval peasants desperately seeking land to cultivate when flat land was in short supply. Most strip lynchets follow the contours, but a few cut across them. Rarely less than 50yd (45m) long, they are commonly 150–200yd (140–180m) often occurring in series, one above another, called 'flights'. Each levelled-out terrace, created only by ploughing, after first removing surface boulders and using them to form the base of a 'riser', is up to 5yd (5.5m) wide and tails off at each end into unploughed land.

Strip lynchets are very difficult to date, and its possible that some may be of Anglian origin, but it seems most likely that they are of medieval origin. What is more certain is that all visible examples in the Dales of strip lynchets, as well as ridge-and-furrow, are now grassed

over as permanent pasture, and have been since the enclosure of fields, so that they have become fossilised survivals of days of peasant ploughing.

Most Dales villages have occupied their present sites for over twelve centuries. A few were established a century after the Conquest as foresters' villages within the Norman hunting forests – Healaugh in Swaledale, Bainbridge in Wensleydale, Buckden in Wharfedale. Deforestation and the removal of land from forest law was a gradual process in which the monasteries played an important role until their power vanished at the Dissolution. In spite of this further woodland clearance which yielded more land for agriculture, the Dales show very few new settlements after the thirteenth century. Some parts of the old forests were enclosed as deer-parks, such as Scale Park above Kettlewell, enclosed by the Nevilles in 1410, and inhabited by wild deer until the eighteenth century.

Both the Anglian and Danish settlers and the medieval colonists had a good eye for a site, choosing well-drained soils above valley flood levels, by beck or river, or on a limestone terrace. Above Reeth, Swaledale villages are at the foot of south-facing slopes: Feetham, Low Row, Gunnerside, Muker and Thwaite at 750–900ft (230–275m), with Keld at 1,000ft (305m), a height distinction shared with Whaw and Marrick. Stalling Busk, above Semerwater, stands at 1,100ft (335m), one of the highest villages in the Dales, but most Wensleydale villages occur in pairs on opposite sides of the valley, at 700–750ft (219–230m) and, significantly, it is around Redmire and Wensley, at 400ft (120m), that the first arable fields occur. Swaledale has no arable land above Richmond.

In Wharfedale, Grassington at 700ft (210m) marks the start of the upper valley, with villages beyond, as well as those in Littondale, at 700–800ft (210–245m), although Oughtershaw, Beckermonds and Halton Gill are above 1,000ft (305m). The former railway settlement at Garsdale Head is close to 1,100ft (335m), but lower down the Settle–Carlisle line, Ribblesdale villages are between 650ft and 900ft (200m and 275m) – for example, Stainforth and Ribble Head. West of the main watershed, Austwick, Clapham and Dent are at about 500ft (150m). Pride of place, however, for height (and sympathy?) goes not to a village but to a pub, Tan Hill Inn, 4 moorland miles above Keld, at 1,732ft (528m) by far the highest permanently occupied building in the

Arncliffe, the main village in Littondale, showing seventeenth- and eighteenth-century buildings round a central green. The original village was Anglian (seventh or eighth century) and built on well-drained gravels

Dales, and indeed the highest inn in Britain.

The surprise is that it has survived for so long. Cam Houses, for long the highest farm in the county, at 1,450ft (440m), is now no longer continuously occupied, although the former drovers' inn at Newby Head 1,400ft (425m), has been a working farm for many years. Many farms and remote cottages, as well as a few villages, have not survived. Of the deserted medieval villages Swaledale claims one, at Ellerton, and Wensleydale four, at East Bolton, West Bolton, Thoresby and Eshington. Most are now represented on the ground by single farms, although Thoresby has two farms. Most were abandoned, for reasons not yet proven, in the fourteenth century. To the south-west of Redmire, at 032897, Thoresby's earthworks are quite clear. A lane from Redmire leads to them, but I found it easier to wade the River Ure, with the water-level low, at Slapestone Wath, and approach from the south via the public bridleway of Stony Stoop Lane. It is possible, with care, to pick out among the mounds and hollows the line of a street, the grassy platforms where houses stood, and the shadowy outline of a small church. There is nothing more, but a rich growth of nettles, the wind in the trees and grazing stock.

In lower Wensleydale, East Witton shows a different story. The main Ripon–Leyburn road touches the eastern end of its neat, mainly rectangular green. The orderly arrangement of cottages along opposite sides of the green, and the commanding situation of St John's church beyond the eastern edge, suggest a planned village. The church, however, is a rebuilding of 1809, replacing the older church of St Martin at Low Thorpe to the south-east, now identified only by its walled-in churchyard, its scattered gravestones and sheltering beeches. A map of 1627 shows St Martin's and seventeen cottages along the near-by lane. Only a handful are there now, settlement having become centred on the green, where today's cottages occupy exactly the same sites as in 1627. Five cottages existing then have since gone, and a row of six across the western end has diminished to two. Thus, the present village is not one of the eighteenth- or nineteenth-century planned settlements, but may well owe its origins and shape to having been planned by the Abbot of Jervaulx around the site of a market established in 1307. Most of the present houses were rebuilt by the squire, the Earl of Ailesbury, at the same time as the church in 1809.

Thus, villages grow or decay, change their position or shape, and react to changing economic tides, but are rarely, if ever, completely static. The granting of market charters, by medieval lords, abbots or squires, influenced trade, the growth of villages, and the development of local roads. Early charters for markets in the Dales include Richmond (1144), Skipton (about the same time, regularised in 1203), Clapham (1201), Wensley (1202), Settle (1249), Sedbergh (1251), Ilkley (1253), Grassington (1281), Carperby (1305), East Witton (1307, when Wensley's was renewed), Appletreewick (1310) and Middleham (1389). Only those in the towns have survived in recent times.

Apart from the natural background of hills, rocks, valleys and rivers, almost all of what is seen today in the Dales' landscape – the pattern of fields with their boundaries of walls or hedges, the farms, villages and small towns – is the product of the past four centuries. Of the buildings in particular, only the castles, tower-houses, monastic ruins and some churches, are older. The events which brought about the change from medieval to 'modern' landscapes started with the Dissolution of the Monasteries, in 1536–39, but even that had, to some extent, been anticipated. As a result of the Dissolution, however, monastic estates were broken up; some were bought by speculators, London merchants or local gentry and leased to existing tenants. Some were for a time retained by the Crown, but eventually were sold to sitting tenants or freeholders – Charles I was frequently short of money, and many royal estates and manors, including the Lordship of Middleham, were sold by the Crown in the 1620s. Lay owners of former monastic property, especially if they had been tenants, had, after two or three generations, saved sufficient capital to build new houses for themselves. Owners of former Crown property needed about the same length of time, so fifty to sixty years after the Dissolution, one of the first of the few 'gentry' houses in the Dales was built. This started the process of rebuilding in stone which continued, with scarcely a break for the Civil War, until the mid-eighteenth century, and, for smaller cottages, another hundred years after that.

4
NEW LANDSCAPES, NEW BUILDINGS

Social changes which gradually evolved during Tudor times, accelerated with the Dissolution of the Monasteries, and continued into the
early seventeenth century, resulted in the decline of the feudal system
and the emergence of the yeoman farmer. In the Dales this development brought about the first period of field enclosures, usually by stone
walls, and the rebuilding in a permanent form, using local stone, of
farmhouses and other buildings which give so distinctive an architectural flavour to the Yorkshire Dales. Visitors to the area are soon aware
of the so-called 'traditional' buildings, recognised as belonging to the
landscape, and which in fact have virtually grown out of it. With the
regrettable exception of modern farm buildings and a few domestic ones
that slipped in before the more rigorous planning controls of the
National Park Authority were applied, most man-made structures in
the Dales look right in their environment.

Only rarely, however, is it a single house that attracts attention.
More often it is the visual appeal of houses in a village, either round a
green as at West Burton, Bainbridge, Linton or Arncliffe, or huddled
close as at Thwaite, Muker, or Kettlewell. In each of these, except
perhaps Linton, few individual houses are outstanding, most being
quite small cottages. Already it is becoming clear that, although there
is a harmony and unity about materials and colours, there is a variation
in styles and sizes. Most are predominantly domestic and rural, rather
than urban; most are vernacular rather than 'polite', a distinction
mooted by Dr R. W. Brunskill, which requires some explanation.

Vernacular buildings are those which are permanent rather than temporary, traditional in design and inspiration rather than academic or formal, made from local materials by local craftsmen, to serve the everyday needs of local people in their homes, farms and simple industries. They are, nevertheless, designed and built with some thought given to their appearance. 'Polite' architecture is more likely to be produced by professional architects, following stylistic rules and often using materials selected to suit these rather than simply making use of what is available nearby.

But the real difference is one of degree and this varies with social status and time. Dales buildings before about 1500 have already been discussed. Anything built between then and about 1650 would have been the houses of wealthier yeomen or less important gentry. From about 1650 to 1750, as wealth gradually spread lower down the social scale, more and more farmers, and an increasing number of professional people – merchants, attorneys, doctors and clergy – built themselves new houses. From the late eighteenth century until about 1860, small cottages were built in villages to house the quarrymen, masons, millworkers and miners. By then, even the smallest houses were beginning to conform to national styles and tastes rather than regional ones.

Swinsty Hall in the Washburn valley, a few miles outside the Park's eastern boundary, was built in 1570 in the fashionable Tudor style, with a hall, originally open to the roof, illuminated by long, mullioned and transomed windows with a string course and hood-moulds. The upper window of a three-storey porch has three sections, the middle one higher than the other two. 'Tripartite' windows like this were built between 1630 and 1670, the idea spreading to Wensleydale, but not, so far as I know, to Swaledale. The porch gable carries a decorative finial repeated at the kneelers of the gable copings. These details are given to illustrate how architectural fashions and idioms entered the Dales, were subsequently copied, and spread – usually from the south and east to the north and west.

Friars Head, Winterburn (932576) was built about 1590 by Stephen Procter, whose forbears were tenants under Fountains and Furness Abbeys before the Dissolution. He later made a fortune, moved to Ripon, and at the end of the century bought the former Fountains Abbey estate, and, in about 1610, built the present Fountains Hall, for which Friars Head must have been a smaller prototype. Now a working farm, Friars Head is a symmetrical, fine late-Tudor house, three storeyed, with mullioned and transomed windows, gables with tripartite windows, adorned with finials. Forty years later when John Colby built his new house, Colby Hall, a mile west of Askrigg, he surely was influenced by Friars Head, although the 1633 building lacks the detail and finesse of Procter's house. Only one other Dales house now survives to show this mainstream influence of late-Tudor style, The Folly at Settle, built as late as 1679, almost a century after Friars Head, by Richard Preston. Undoubtedly, Ribblesdale must have been as conservative as anywhere in the Dales, but some details of the house incorporated ideas then being used by Wren on his new London churches. The Folly's most striking features are its huge run of ground-floor windows and its rich doorways. Old Hall, Askrigg, contemporary with The Folly, was similar to it, though smaller and less ostentatious, and had a balcony and upper doors added in the eighteenth century. Unfortunately, it was destroyed by fire fifty years ago and nothing remains of William Thornton's fine house.

Also in Wensleydale, but at the lower end of the valley, Braithwaite Hall near East Witton (117858), now in the care of the National Trust, is a working farmhouse, broadly contemporary with The Folly and Askrigg Old Hall. Dating from 1667 it is flat fronted, with three low-pitched gables containing oval windows, while windows on the two main floors are stone-mullioned.

Near Appletreewick in Wharfedale, Parcevall Hall, now used as a Bradford diocesan retreat, is a former yeoman farmhouse, probably built in the early seventeenth century. Restored and extended in 1928, it still retains late Tudor characteristics. In Appletreewick itself, High Hall of similar date was restored by Sir William Craven and is a three-storeyed house with a porch originally of two storeys. It was Sir William who in 1602 built and endowed the grammar school in nearby Burnsall, which continued as a grammar school until 1876, and is now the primary school for the village. In appearance it is identical to a small manor-house, two storeyed with a gabled porch, mullioned windows and gables with finials. It can be regarded almost as a blueprint for two generations of houses of similar size and style, built by prosperous yeomen in the Dales during the first half of the seventeenth century, with only small variations from one part of the Dales to another, yet usually quite easy to recognise.

At Malham, Hill Top Farm has a 1617 date stone, stone-mullioned windows and a gabled porch, while Calamine House, formerly a warehouse for the mines on Malham Moor, on the west side of the road opposite Town Head, has its mullioned windows blocked up. A crumbling date stone above the back door suggests 1672, although 1612 is a more likely reading, judging by the architectural features surviving.

One of the finest yeomen's houses of the seventeenth century is Ingman Lodge, formerly a Furness Abbey grange (780780). Now called Lodge Hall, it lies just off the Horton road a mile south of Ribble Head, a remote situation for a large, three-storey house. Christopher Weatherhead rebuilt or enlarged it considerably in 1687. His initials and the date appear above the very elaborate doorway, whose decorations include a halberd carved on each side, a feature also occurring at Hanlith Hall near Malham and New Hall, Settle.

Externally at least, Old Hall, Thoralby (995866), built in 1641, shows all the characteristic features of early-seventeenth-century Dales houses, built of coursed rubble, with squared quoins, stone-mullioned casement windows, a gabled, two-storey porch whose doorway has a 'four-centred' arch, a carved lintel, drip-moulds, and small pinnacles on gables. Details of this house have been given to allow it to be used as a reference against which other Dales houses can be identified and possibly dated. But in exploring the area to seek its best vernacular architecture it needs to be remembered that houses change almost every generation. While most changes are probably internal and take into account the increasing desire for convenience and comfort, outside appearances have altered too, especially height, the number and size of windows, and doorways. When new staircases were added, for example, additional windows might be constructed at the rear. Materials, however, did not change and the continued use of stone quarried locally has contributed to the harmony of Dales buildings in their setting.

In the northern dales and much of Wharfedale, sandstone is almost exclusively used both for walling and roofs. As explained in an earlier chapter, the Yoredale Series of rocks in these areas contain a number of sandstone strata, and stone from one layer is more suited to walls, from another for roofs. The use of stones from different strata with slight differences in colour and texture has given to most vernacular buildings a particularly lively patina. For dressings round doors and windows, and for the all-important quoins at corners, gritstone was preferred. This is more massive, rougher and can be cleanly cut. In Wharfedale below Grassington a gritstone was used for walls of houses, and, lacking the variety of sandstones, it has produced houses of more uniform colour and texture, at Burnsall and Threshfield in particular.

In the villages and farms of upper Wharfedale, Littondale, Ribblesdale and around Malham, where limestone predominates, this has been used as building material. Less easily worked than the other stones it can, nevertheless, be shaped roughly, making it suitable for rubble walling. But, being less resistant to weathering, it benefits from a protective covering, so house walls have been given a rendered finish of lime plaster or limewash. Houses at Malham, Arncliffe, Hawkswick, Stainforth and Langcliffe illustrate this while, in the Settle area, whitewashed walls create startling highlights among the more muted tones of their neighbours. Sandstone flags or, in Ribblesdale, Horton slates, were used for roofs, and gritstone was still preferred for quoins and dressings.

Whitewash also prevails in the western valleys, where surface treatment was necessary to protect and give a smoother finish to walls of older, harder, slaty rocks. The influence of Cumbria and the Lake District shows itself not only in landscape but in the buildings, as becomes increasingly apparent in a journey down Garsdale or any exploration in Dentdale. In these two valleys, the scattered farms are usually whitewashed, although their associated buildings are almost invariably left unrendered. Dent itself is a tight-knit cluster of whitewashed houses and cottages, roofed with dark sandstone flags. Cobbled streets add to the delights of textural contrast.

To return to individual buildings, those so far mentioned have been the houses of yeomen and lesser gentry. The spread of farm building in the seventeenth century has yielded a rich legacy throughout the Dales, both as isolated farmsteads and within villages, and it is these, with others added in the first quarter of the following century, which dictate the vernacular architectural character of the district. A common, though not universal, feature of this seventeenth-century rebuilding of Dales houses is dating and initialling (with the initials of the owner and his wife) by carved panels over doorways or windows. Although they do not all authenticate that a particular house was built at that date, for some may represent a date of addition or alteration, they do form a guide. Of over 150 dated houses surveyed, mainly in Wensleydale and Swaledale, more than half were built between 1600 and 1699, and nearly a quarter between 1700 and 1760. The period 1650–99 shows twice as many houses as any other fifty-year period, with a peak around 1680–90.

Common to all the Dales is the 'long-house' profile, buildings of two or three bays, only one room deep, with cowshed and barn adjoining the living accommodation under one very long, low-pitched roof. West New House, at the head of Bishopdale (965837), exemplifies this style. Dated 1635, with long, low, stone-mullioned windows with a continuous drip-mould above, a central stack, and a stair turret at the back probably added later, it shows on close inspection another feature. Its walls were apparently raised by 2–3ft (60–90cm), probably in the

Sixteenth-century hall-house at Burton Hill, Dent, which was extended and altered in 1655. The upper window on the left is oak mullioned. The small building on the right was the wash-house

West New House, Bishopdale, dated 1635. Note the long, low, deeply recessed stone-mullioned windows, with continuous drip-mould above. The roof-line was originally lower, and the roof was probably thatched when the house was built

early eighteenth century, and an old ling-thatched roof of steeper pitch replaced by a roof of stone slates and a shallow pitch – 30–35°. Most early- to mid-seventeenth-century houses in the Dales were originally thatched, and when the thatch was replaced the new stone roofs demanded a shallower pitch. So walls were heightened and, probably at the same time, the upper chamber, previously open to the rafters, was ceiled over, making a one-and-a-half storey house into a two-storey one. Early upper rooms, or chambers, were often only lit by a small window above the door, and many of these survive, as at West New House.

Remarkably little is known about these seventeenth-century houses. Old inventories frequently refer to them as 'fire houses', that is, houses with one or more hearths, thus differentiating them from cow-houses or barns. Many also possessed a fire-window, a feature that persisted until about 1720. This was a small window at the hearth end of the main room or hall, illuminating the dark corner by a big, stone-hooded fireplace. It can be identified today by its size (although it may have been enlarged) and position, aligned with the main chimney-stack, and sometimes paralleled by a matching window in the chamber above. Fire-windows seem to be more common in isolated farmhouses than in village houses, although Bolton Dean (c1700), near the Wensleydale Heifer Inn in West Witton, has one, as do houses in the hamlet of Countersett, above Bainbridge.

The two-storey porch, sometimes with a tripartite window, is a feature of Countersett Hall, Old Cotes in Arncliffe (both 1650) and the old manor-house at Bainbridge (1670), much altered last century. However, the most impressive example is at Threshfield, where the seventeenth-century manor-house, also greatly altered, retains a superb three-storey porch with a six-light window on the first floor and a Tudor rose-window above. Nearby is a barn, dated 1661, with three doorways, while in Arncliffe a characteristic Littondale barn with a small porch has the date 1666 over its entrance.

Space has allowed me to mention only a few examples of vernacular buildings of the period 1600–1720. Their characteristics have been described so that similar buildings may be identified throughout the area. Others will be referred to in the Gazetteer, but it may be worth pointing out that, for reasons not fully understood, certain parts of the Dales and certain villages are richer in seventeenth-century building than others. Bishopdale is particularly good for farmhouses, as are the areas around Bainbridge and Malham. Although Low Oxnop (931974) is Swaledale's most impressive house of this date, Grinton village has some good vernacular buildings, while the villages of Grassington,

Low Oxnop Hall, near Muker, Swaledale, built by John and Elizabeth Alderson in 1685. Note the stone-mullioned windows, those in the upper floor with transoms. The two pairs of small 'fire-windows' indicate back-to-back fireplaces in the principal rooms, with a large central chimney stack above. This is probably the best seventeenth-century house in Swaledale

Conistone, Arncliffe and Malham are rewarding. It is, however, Linton which must be visited to see where new architectural ideas probably first infiltrated the Dales, a century after Inigo Jones had introduced the classical Palladian style of building in London.

Architects who developed these fashions of balance, symmetry and ostentatious detail included Wren, Hawksmoor and Vanbrugh, and by the end of the seventeenth century they were becoming widespread nationally. Fountaine Hospital in Linton was probably the first Dales building designed according to these principles. Sir John Fountaine, a good example of the local boy who went to London and made a fortune, and who almost certainly met both Hawksmoor and Vanbrugh there, left in his will of 1721 sufficient money to build and endow an almshouse in his native village. Vanbrugh had earlier designed a small almshouse for Enfield, near London, which was never built, and it is thought that this design was used at Linton.

By Vanbrugh's standards it is modest and its only local features are
the materials from which it is built, mainly gritstone from the nearby
Thorpe Fell quarries. Special prominence is given to the quoins, the
pilasters of the central tower each side of the entrance, a Palladian window above the door, pediments and a cupola, and heavy 'Gibbs' surrounds to the windows. Ground-floor windows are tall with vertical
sashes, first-floor ones square with horizontally sliding sashes, with
white-painted wooden bars breaking up the glazed area into small
panes. A building such as this, professionally designed, impressively
formal, is not vernacular, so the period which followed its completion
represents a watershed in Dales building styles. The new ideas spread
outwards from Linton, taken up by rural builders and adapted to suit
local needs, within the more limited means of local people.

Almost every village and market town shows examples of the attractive Georgian style which continued, in various sizes and modified
forms, until as late as the 1860s. In Linton itself, the Old Hall and the
present Linton House, each a seventeenth-century structure, were
added to or altered to accommodate the new fashion. Old Hall is particularly worth noting, for much of the original building was left un-

Linton Old Hall, Wharfedale. The eighteenth-century wing on the right, with its
tall windows and decorated doorway, was added to the seventeenth-century house
on the left, with its long, low windows

touched, but the eastern end was rebuilt in about 1750 in a three-storey Georgian style, albeit not a wholly classical one, for window arrangements are not balanced and two of them retain stone mullions and transoms. Rather more 'pure' Georgian houses can be seen in near-by Thorpe, Cracoe and Rylstone, while in Grassington, a Mr Brown, one of the promoters of the Grassington to Pateley Bridge turnpike road, built the elegant Grassington House, now an hotel, in 1760. In upper Wharfedale, one of the farms at Yockenthwaite was rebuilt at about the same time.

These eighteenth-century houses are easily recognised by reason of the 'boxier' appearance, their greater height and depth. Taller windows illuminated taller rooms, both on the ground floor and first floor; houses were two rooms deep, with a central stairway rising from a hall behind a central doorway, and then turning back on itself at a half-landing lit by a tall, often round-headed window at the back of the house. Details were kept simple, the windows usually having only plain surrounds and sills, although occasional mouldings introduced an element of ostentation. Quoins were flush with walls and generally an ashlared stone (smooth-dressed) was used. Such houses were the houses of an emergent middle class of prosperous farmers, traders, merchants, mine-owners, and professional people such as clergy, doctors and attorneys.

The traditional Dales vernacular – the long, narrow house – was adapted to incorporate the new ideas into existing structures from the mid-eighteenth century onwards. Walls were often raised, upper rooms ceiled over and a new roof replaced the original thatch. Long, low windows were replaced by tall ones with vertical sashes giving 'uneasy' façades. Increasing prosperity made it possible to satisfy the desire for greater privacy by, for example, the transfer of the cooking process from the general living-room to a kitchen added on at the back of the house, accommodated beneath the familiar 'outshut'. Giving this an extra floor provided an additional bedroom space, reached by a new staircase, this in turn requiring the insertion of the characteristic half-landing window, usually the clue to a late eighteenth- or early-nineteenth-century addition. The house I have lived in for ten years was recently surveyed by members of the North Yorkshire and Cleveland Vernacular Buildings Study Group, who identified at least eight separate changes and developments since it was built in about 1700 as a one-bay, one-and-a-half storey, thatched house. In this, it is by no means exceptional, and illustrates the earlier assertion that houses change. In spite of the introduction of classical ideas, the Dales vernacular has not been swamped and there is still a rich heritage of traditional buildings.

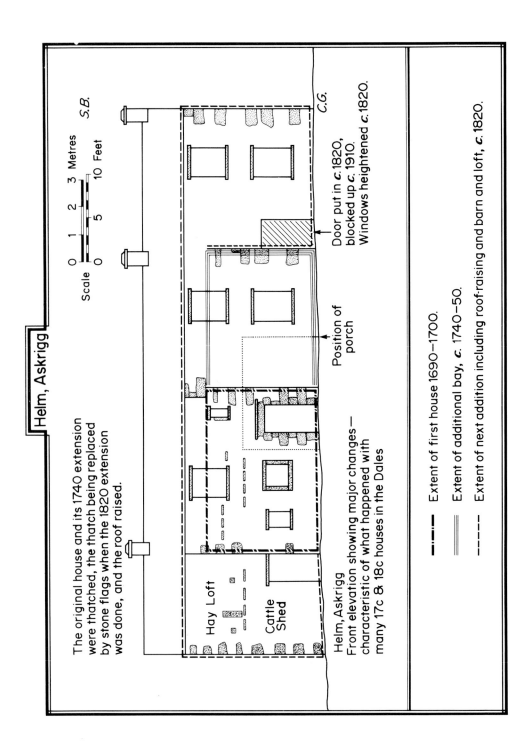

Helm, Askrigg

The original house and its 1740 extension were thatched, the thatch being replaced by stone flags when the 1820 extension was done, and the roof raised.

Scale

0 1 2 3 Metres

0 5 10 Feet

S.B.

C.G.

Door put in *c*.1820, blocked up *c*.1910. Windows heightened *c*.1820.

Position of porch

Hay Loft

Cattle Shed

Helm, Askrigg
Front elevation showing major changes — characteristic of what happened with many 17c & 18c houses in the Dales

— · — · Extent of first house 1690–1700.

||||| Extent of additional bay, *c*. 1740–50.

– – – – Extent of next addition including roof-raising and barn and loft, *c*. 1820.

Contemporary with the new developments in houses came a steady growth in the labouring and artisan population, which continued until the middle of last century, largely as a result of the expansion of the lead-mining industry and the introduction of water-powered mills producing woollen and cotton goods. Increased demand for new housing was met by the construction – by employers, landowners and labourers themselves – of small cottages, sometimes in terraces, or sometimes by the patching-up of existing crude hovels. Much of this building or re-building took the form of infilling existing spaces in villages, thus creating the almost continuous street frontages such as those at West Witton, Carperby, Askrigg, Gunnerside, Kettlewell, Austwick and many others. The larger early-nineteenth-century cottage was basically a scaled-down version of a Georgian house; smaller ones simply halved this to provide a kitchen-parlour and rear scullery downstairs and two bedrooms above. These were the houses which were abandoned, often becoming derelict, when mill-work, mining and quarrying ceased. The same cottages became second homes and holiday cottages from the late 1950s onwards. Now, the supply has dried up and these same cottages change hands at £25,000 or more – much more if they have a little land and a good view.

Although many of these smaller houses and cottages dating from the first half of last century have shadowy hints of Georgian fashion, they are essentially vernacular. Numerically, they contribute significantly to the rural scene, justifying the description of villages as being attractive, if austere. If you examine any village view closely, it soon becomes obvious that only a few houses are of outstanding architectural merit. Yet the mixture as a unit is satisfying, providing visual evidence of a former community as well as of a way of life that has vanished. Almost certainly today's occupants of village houses are considerably more prosperous than any of the earlier generations who lived and worked in the Dales.

Mention has been made of turnpike roads. From 1751 to 1853 a series of turnpike Acts was promoted in the Dales, leading not only to an increase in travel, trade and prosperity, but also to the urbanising of many villages, largely through the building of hotels and coaching inns, often of three storeys and with imposing façades. These play a part in the appeal of streets in Reeth, Middleham, Askrigg, Hawes and Grassington, while the market towns of Richmond, Leyburn, Sedbergh and Settle owe much of their character to the dignified hotels and inns of the turnpike days. In one respect, the second half of the eighteenth century and the first quarter of the nineteenth could be regarded as the zenith of Dales prosperity, agriculture, industry and social life. This period was also the high noon of changes in farming practices which have given us the wall-patterned landscapes of valleys and hillsides that are such integral features of the Dales scene today.

The process of enclosure, in which the common fields of townships and villages were divided into small, separate fields under individual ownership and walled off one from another, had been slowly developing through the seventeenth and early eighteenth centuries. A survey in 1605 of the lordship of Middleham, covering the south side of Wensleydale between Wensley and Hawes, showed that most of the best valley land had been enclosed, but not completely divided into individually owned fields. On the lower fell-slopes were large, enclosed pastures, some of several hundred acres in extent, these being 'stinted' or controlled pastures where inhabitants of townships had the right to graze specified numbers of cattle or sheep. Above these stinted pastures were the upland commons and wastes, where individual farmers could graze any numbers of stock, although this was usually limited to the number they could feed on their normal winter hay crops.

Common fields still existed. The three common fields of West Witton comprised 120 acres (48ha), four at West Burton 125 acres (50ha) and three at Carlton-in-Coverdale 113 acres (45ha). The survey showed that other villages in the area also retained common fields, so an open-field agriculture persisted in Wensleydale, and a similar pattern of land use doubtless prevailed throughout the Dales. The purpose of enclosing meadow and pasture was to improve stock management by allowing more control over grazing – and therefore the dung produced – and breeding. Enclosures of the seventeenth century were done by local agreement, involving individual landowners selling or exchanging their strip holdings in the open fields, sometimes with an agreement to build walls. At Grassington, when this occurred in about 1605, the result was that the formerly open west field was divided into a series of long, walled enclosures of different widths, but still related in shape to the original plough strips from which they had evolved.

The straight-walled fields creating the familiar rectilinear pattern of Dales landscapes are the result of Parliamentary enclosures which took place in the area mainly between 1760 and 1830. These originated from the desire of leading landowners in the parish or township to enclose the remaining open fields. In order to do so and thus eliminate the small peasant holdings, they had to petition Parliament, which would subsequently pass an Enclosure Act for the parish, apportioning strips of meadow, plough and common. While the Enclosure Awards led to the more efficient use of land and better farming, it is doubtful if they brought much, if any, benefit to the peasants, and what the poorer part of the community thought about them is not usually recorded.

Many Enclosure Awards included clauses which allowed for limekilns to be built near suitable outcrops of limestone, as well as for the retention of parish and township quarries from which local people could continue freely to obtain stone for houses and roofs. Stone for the actual field walls came initially from field clearance, but mostly from small quarries as close as possible to where the stone was to be used. In the limestone area, limestone was used exclusively; in the northern dales, it was sandstone; and in those dales where the Yoredale rocks occur, both types of stone were used for walling, sometimes within a short stretch of wall as it crossed from one stratum to another. Wensleydale shows this particularly well, just as it also shows the use of field clearance materials, or river boulders, the latter identified by the rounded appearance of individual stones, the result of smoothing by glaciers or water.

Rylstone's common pastures were enclosed in 1772, the remaining common fields at Grassington in 1788, and Linton's five years later. The fields of Kettlewell and Conistone were walled in about 1800, and Malham's fields had almost completely been patterned with miles of limestone walls by the end of the century. In Wensleydale, some of Aysgarth's pastures and upland commons were enclosed in 1777, and over the next forty years successive Enclosure Acts gradually brought about the present field pattern, with walls and hedges, of lower Bishop-dale as well as around Carperby. Further up the dale Askrigg's township fields were enclosed soon after the Napoleonic Wars, in about 1817–20. Although some Swaledale parishes (eg Fremington) were enclosed in about 1780, most of the enclosures were carried out during the early nineteenth century. That familiar, well-loved landscape on Reeth Moor, seen so well from above Grinton, is the result of its 1826 Enclosure Award. Near the head of the dale, Muker and Kisdon Pasture were walled in 1832.

Thus, much of the Dales field pattern was man-made, its creation spanning about fifty years, during which time hundreds of miles of walls were built. Enclosure Acts specified their construction, giving a height of 5–6ft, (1.5–1.8m), a base about 3ft (90cm) wide narrowing to 1½ft (45cm) at the top, each being a two-skin wall with a carefully packed filling of small stones and pebbles. Each rood (7yd/6.4m) contained twenty-one 'throughs' or stretchers laid in two or three rows across the two skins, usually projecting at each side. These acted as ties, holding the sides together, a system also used in the walls of houses and barns.

Later Awards around the middle of last century enclosed some of the out-pasture of the moors. These produced the long straight walls arrowing up the hillsides or contouring the edge of the waste. The exciting road from Arncliffe to Malham shows these sturdily aggressive landscape features to perfection. One outcome of the Enclosure Awards was the need to wall the old roads and trackways, the drove roads, packhorse routes and the more recent turnpikes. There was also the need to create new roads whereby landowners and others with common rights could continue to have access to the upland commons, to graze their stock and to dig peat. Retention of the 'peat roads', in fact, is a regular feature of the Awards, and appropriate names occur repeatedly on the large-scale maps – Peat Moor Lane, Moor Road, Common Lane, Intake Lane and Accommodation Road. Dent's Enclosure Award of 1859 was one of the last in the Dales and one of its features is the Occupation Road which contours, as a walled but unsurfaced lane, from Deepdale Head (724824) to the Barbondale road (680863).

Unfortunately, walls collapse. Sheep are prone to jumping over them, lambs rather like standing on them. Occasionally – far less frequently than accusations imply – visitors climb them. My own impressions are that farm vehicles, bulk milk tankers, and livestock wagons probably cause most damage, certainly to walls bordering narrow farm lanes and tracks. Whatever the cause, the extent of stone walls in the Dales is diminishing yearly. Few craftsmen wallers are available to repair or replace them. While many farmers sensibly try to repair walls as soon as they show signs of neglect which could quickly lead to collapse, others, with less time, inclination or skill, prefer to fill a gap with an old gate, or, if there is a substantial stretch of wall involved, to repair it with post-and-wire fencing. This is much cheaper than walling and is easier to repair or replace, but it gives no shelter to ewes or lambs. Thus, finance and expediency contribute to the loss of stone walls and their replacement by non-traditional materials. We shall all be the losers. Ironically, some of the best new walls occur where road improvements are carried out. Old walls are knocked down, roads widened, and the highway authorities build new walls, using traditional materials and methods, even if the 'throughs' are too uniform and the capping stones are mortared on. Good examples can be seen in Ribblesdale and upper Wensleydale.

It is probable that most of the field barns of the Dales are contemporary with the enclosure walls, that is, 120–200 years old. A few are undoubtedly older, judging by their date stones and appearance. Taken

Barn at Town Head, Thoralby, with the line of former cruck-frame construction very distinct. The barn would then have been thatched

together it is the combination of stone barns and stone-walled fields which forms the most memorable aspect of the Dales landscape and makes it unique in Britain, possibly in Europe. Nobody knows how many barns there are in the area because nobody has taken the trouble to count them. In a view from the Pennine Way just above Muker in Swaledale I have counted eighty, and the 1:25,000 OS map shows about a hundred within a half-mile radius of the village. If you multiply that figure many times, it becomes apparent that there must be several hundred throughout the Dales. I should expect the total to exceed two thousand. It is not surprising that the traveller Richard Pococke, who visited the area in 1751, was so amazed to see what he described as 'houses built in most of the fields', that were 'unusual and uncommon'.

Yet that was before the enclosures. What he saw would have been small, simple structures, built of wood or stone and ling-thatched. Today's barns are their replacements, just as today's houses have replaced simpler, cruder structures.

Barns are and were wholly functional, designed to store hay grown in and collected from the near-by hay-meadows and to house cattle during the winter months – November to late April or early May. Their names vary. In Swaledale they are called cow-houses or field-houses (when built away from the farm). In Wensleydale they are barns or laithes – a name more commonly used in Wharfedale and the Craven area. Cattle occupy the shippon or, in Nidderdale, the mistral. Hay-storage is in the loft. Swaledale barns and cow-houses tend to be smaller and simpler than elsewhere, while those in Wensleydale show a variety of sizes. In upper Wharfedale and Littondale laithes are architecturally more impressive, often having porches with double doors allowing wheeled carts to unload their contents of hay or corn under cover. Corn was commonly grown in the Craven dales, and a number of laithes had threshing-floors aligned with the porch, with cow-standings and hay-mew (where hay was stacked) on either side of this stone floor.

In the northern dales barns are two-storeyed, rectangular in plan, one or two bays wide (16–30ft/4.9–9.1m) and one bay deep (14–15ft/4.3–4.6m), with two or three doors at the front giving access to the shippon and hay-mews. Above, and at the side or more usually the back, especially if a barn is built at right angles to a slope, is the forking hole by which hay was forked from cart or sledge into the hay-loft, a job now done by elevators lifting hay-bales. Many Swaledale barns stored hay from floor almost to roof, but elsewhere hay-lofts were more common. Where possible, barns were erected where there was a rise in the land, not only because it was obviously drier but also because the spreading of accumulated manure from them was done more easily down a slope, but it was not unduly difficult to bring the hay from the field up a slope. It is quite common to see a number of barns, well separated, but aligned at the same level along the lower slopes of a hillside, representing the greatest height at which hay could successfully be grown. One very characteristic sequence can easily be seen south of Gayle, near Hawes, at about the 1,000ft (305m) contour.

Now, however, farming is less labour intensive, and large modern multi-span cowsheds, electrically heated, easier to clean, and situated close to the farm, house a whole herd of cattle and their feed over the winter. The old barns, with room for four to eight beasts, each structure the centre of its own winter farming operations for six months of the year, are becoming increasingly redundant. They are merely used for general storage or for nothing at all. The problem is, what to do with them?

Where barns are situated within villages and thus easily connected to the services of the main utilities, they can be and have been converted to residential use, some rather more sympathetically than others. Conistone and Hawkswick have good examples, while the well-known 'Wesley's Barn' in Grassington, with its 1683 date panel, has a new lease of life as an outdoor-sports equipment centre, but has successfully retained most of its original features, including arched ventilation slits in the walls, and pigeon-holes. So far as the isolated field barns are concerned, resources are not available to safeguard all those that are now redundant, although the National Park Authority would like to preserve representative examples. A few have been converted to provide low-cost visitor accommodation of the self-catering hostel type; barns at Catholes near Sedbergh, Cam Houses and Barden Tower received financial help for conversions of this type from the Countryside Commission, while the National Park Committee has helped at Dub Cote near Horton-in-Ribblesdale and Grange Farm at Hubberholme. Local farmers benefit from the overnight fees (in 1985 about £3 per person), and visitors appreciate this additional accommodation. The Council for Small Industries in Rural Areas (CoSIRA) has announced the availability of grants for the conversion of some barns to light industrial use. If the National Park Committee is actually prepared to implement this offer, some additional local employment might arise, which would benefit Dales residents rather than visitors.

Three barns close to where I live are completely derelict. This end result is not difficult to achieve. A few loose slates in the roof are first ignored; rain, wind and weather begin to wreak havoc, slowly at first, then with increasing effect. Within a few years at the most the roof has gone. Then comes the attack on the walls. Man's contribution to the process need be no more than simple neglect. Yet a few simple and relatively cheap roof repairs in the first place could have prevented the dereliction. The old adage needs to be remembered: 'For the want of a nail the shoe was lost . . .' The National Park Committee now makes grants available for the repair and improvement of traditional stone buildings; grants are also available for the demolition of eyesores. It may be necessary, in order to conserve so important a feature of the landscape and architectural heritage of the Dales, to try to tap EEC resources.

A few barns, usually in remote places and likely to be seen only by walkers, have part of their upper floor space adapted for living accom-

modation, with a hearth and chimney. These 'bothies' were probably
used as shepherds' shelters, especially during lambing, in the same way
as small, wheeled huts were used by downland shepherds in the chalk
country of southern England. Bothies in the Dales are rare, and those
which I know are in danger of becoming derelict. A much smaller type
of stone structure in the fields is a 'hogg-house'. These single-storey
buildings with one or two doors provided shelter in bad winter weather
for 'hoggs' – April lambs experiencing their first winter are by this time
known as hoggs.

Vernacular buildings are an irreplaceable record of the social history
of the Dales. There is little doubt that a high proportion of visitors
come to the area as much to see and enjoy its unspectacular architectural heritage as its scenic splendours. Very little printed or published
information exists to explain the significance of specific features, a gap
which urgently needs filling. The Department of the Environment has
a procedure for 'listing' buildings of special architectural or historic
interest, and this is the main way of protecting individual or small
groups of buildings. Ironically, only that part of the National Park in
the South Lakeland District of Cumbria has an up-to-date list. The
larger area, covered by the Richmondshire and Craven Districts of
North Yorkshire, is still without recent lists.

The National Park Committee has a statutory duty to consider desig-
nating Conservation Areas in villages and towns for the purpose of pre-
serving and enhancing them. A number of villages in the Craven and
Sedbergh Districts have Conservation Areas – Appletreewick,
Arncliffe, Bolton Abbey, Buckden, Burnsall, Clapham, Dent, Grassington, Hubberholme, Ingleton, Kettlewell, Langcliffe, Linton, Sedbergh, Settle and Starbotton. In the Richmondshire District only
Hudswell, near Richmond, has a designation. Local opposition from
other villages has so far prevented any Conservation Areas being designated in Swaledale and Wensleydale. One can only wonder what the
parish councils concerned expect to gain by such an attitude. If Askrigg
is anything to go by, designation might have prevented one particular
conversion which was rightly singled out by the late Alec Clifton-
Taylor as being visually disastrous. To quote him, it 'suffers from grotes-
quely unsuitable fenestration and a poor little door'. The fenestration
includes leaded lights and some stained glass.

If this example gains a black mark, examples from other villages are
more encouraging and underline the advantage of Conservation Area
status, with the added advantage of financial and sometimes practical
help. Re-cobbling, tree planting, and the long-overdue underground-

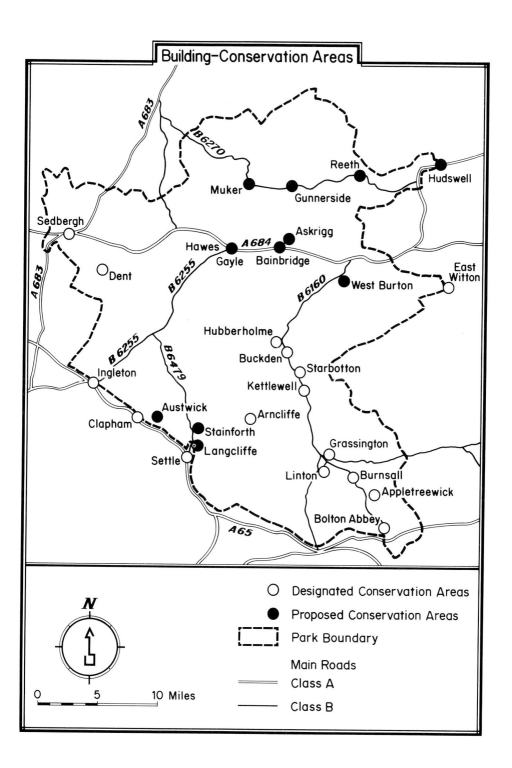

Building-Conservation Areas

A683

B6270

Reeth

Muker

Gunnerside

Hudswell

Sedbergh

Askrigg

Hawes   A684

Dent   Gayle   Bainbridge

A683

B6255

B6160   West Burton   East Witton

Hubberholme

B6255

Buckden

B6479

Starbotton

Ingleton

Kettlewell

Austwick

Clapham

Arncliffe

Stainforth

Langcliffe

Settle

Grassington

Linton   Burnsall

Appletreewick

Bolton Abbey

A65

N

0   5   10 Miles

○ Designated Conservation Areas

● Proposed Conservation Areas

▭ Park Boundary

Main Roads

═ Class A

— Class B

ing of electric power lines have helped to improve a number of village-scapes. Villages with greens are particularly vulnerable to motor-car invasion. Most greens are registered as common land and cannot be developed, but haphazard parking of vehicles can ruin the important sward, so the parish councils concerned rightly adopt a no-parking-on-the-green policy. But other open spaces in villages are often an integral part of their character and these also need to be zealously safeguarded.

Unfortunately, no such safeguards prevent the proliferation of large, unsightly agricultural buildings. As Marion Shoard pointed out in 1980, 'Farmers' freedom to transform the countryside is enormous.' A farmer can erect any building without having to apply for planning permission, provided it is less than 5,000sq ft (464.5m²) in ground floor area, less than 40ft (12m) high, at least 80ft (24m) from a metalled road and at least 100yd (91m) from another building. Five thousand square feet is larger than two tennis-courts, and tower silos, of which there are a few now in the Dales, are designed to be just under 40ft high. Any householder requires planning permission for even a small building or change to his or her house, a regulation even more stringently applied (in theory) in National Parks. One scarcely begrudges farmers wanting to make their working conditions more convenient; the huge structures they erect should, at least, be given a coat of dark paint – brown or dull green – to disguise the monstrosities a bit.

Ingleborough from Scales Moor, near Ingleton. The water-worn limestone at a shake-hole with limestone pavement beyond are features of the Karst landscape, contrasting with Ingleborough's millstone-grit cap

5
INDUSTRIAL ARCHAEOLOGY

Pastoral farming has always been the main occupation in the Yorkshire Dales. Other industries, however, have left their scars, particularly the extractive processes of stone-quarrying, lead-mining and to a lesser extent, coal-mining. Large-scale quarrying, mainly of limestone, continues at Giggleswick, Helwith Bridge, Horton-in-Ribblesdale, Kilnsey, Swinden and Redmire. Additionally, a consistently good supply of water in rivers and their tributaries encouraged the building of small, water-powered corn- and cloth-mills up to the early nineteenth century, their use continuing into the days of steam power.

These old industries rarely overlapped. Stone was quarried from hillsides, gritstone usually from higher up the fells. Most sites where coal or lead was mined were located near the heads of remote tributary valleys or on the high moors where the remains of old workings add to, rather than detract from, the austere beauty of their wilderness setting. Indeed, the traveller in these lonely places sees from the road very little evidence of old industries. Terminal stacks on skylines at Cobscar, above Redmire, and on Malham and Grassington Moors, merely serve as visual pointers to past centuries of human toil. Many mill buildings, too, have vanished, become derelict or been converted to other uses. Old quarries have become grassed over or are full of nettles; some are

Semerwater from above Countersett. This is the largest natural lake in the Dales, easily reached from Bainbridge in Wensleydale official tips, others unofficially so. Scattered boulders or spoil-heaps reveal locations, while dressing-floors and a few ruined buildings confirm the sites, many named as 'Quarry' on the original OS 6in maps of the 1850s.

Mills

Documentary evidence suggests that in medieval times almost every village in the Dales had a water corn-mill, timber-built and each serving the needs of only a few families. If a greater output was needed, extra water-wheels were used, as at Ulshaw, below Middleham, where in 1746 there were 'three mills under one roof'. Such 'subsistence milling' was sufficient for an agricultural economy but inadequate for the growing market towns and larger villages of the late eighteenth century, so many mills were rebuilt then, incorporating new technological improvements. It is these buildings which survive, many on the sites of earlier structures. When flour became more readily available from local markets, imported from big steam-driven mills at large ports, small local corn-mills went out of use, sometimes being adapted or again rebuilt as cotton-spinning mills.

A number of textile mills in the Dales were purpose-built in the late eighteenth century. Gayle Mill, near Hawes (872895) is, externally, one of the least changed, a three-storey, six-bay structure of 1784, built as a cotton-mill but soon turned to the woollen trade. *White's Directory* of 1840 refers to it as a 'worsted mill'. Near-by houses in the village, along Beckstones, were built as combing and carding woolshops. Clints House, in the middle of them, was the home of the Rouths, builders of Gayle Mill. Several years later it became a saw-mill, and more recently has been used as a joiner's shop and builder's store. In the early nineteenth century two mills were built adjoining Gayle Beck in Hawes, one on the east side in the tall building which is now a shop. When a second mill was built shortly afterwards on the west side the original one became a dye-house. The later structure continued as a woollen-mill until early this century when it became the Wensleydale Cheese Dairy of Edward Chapman.

Gayle Beck is a good example of the way in which several mills utilised the flow of water of a relatively modest stream. At Askrigg the

Gayle Mill, near Hawes. It was built in 1784 as a cotton mill, but soon turned to woollen goods. Later it became a saw-mill, and is now a joiner's shop and store. The tail-race of the wheel can be seen at water-level

waters of Mill Gill powered three mills; West Mill, the original corn-mill, continued to produce oatmeal until the 1930s and was then converted to provide the village with an early electricity supply. Lower down the water's course are the buildings – now a private house – of a former cotton-mill, later a flax-mill, while near the road is Low Mill which made worsted yarn before it became a saw-mill. A few years ago it gained a new lease of life through being extended and converted by the Askrigg Foundation into a residential youth centre, with special facilities recently added to allow it to accommodate handicapped people.

One of the best-known of Wensleydale's mills is at Aysgarth. Just below the bridge Yore Mill was originally built in 1784 for worsted yarn, but soon turned to cotton-spinning. Its long mill-leat, controlled by small sluice-gates, channelled water on the south side of the river from just above the Upper Falls to power an internal water-wheel, and the tailrace is still readily recognised near river level at the mill's lower end. When the Hon John Byng, later Lord Torrington, visited Aysgarth in 1792 he did not like what he saw. Never one to mince words, he wrote:

What has completed the destruction of every rural thought has been the erection of a cotton-mill on one side, whereby prospect and quiet are destroyed . . . here now is a great flaring mill, whose back stream has drawn off half the water of the falls above the bridge. With the bell ringing, and the clamour of the mill, all the vale is disturbed.

But the mill which so affronted him had a short life. Thirty years later the Richmondshire historian T. D. Whitaker apparently felt some degree of satisfaction 'at the sight of a ruined cotton-mill, which had once intruded itself upon this beautiful scene'. However, the mill may have been repaired soon after his visit, for an 1823 *Directory* refers to three corn-millers and a millwright at Aysgarth, although these could have been at Aysgarth Mill, now derelict, some way above the Upper Falls.

When Yore Mill was advertised for sale in 1851, it was described as a 'commodious Water Corn Mill 4 storeys high, with rooms 58 feet long and 28 feet wide, the two lower ones used as a corn mill . . . and the upper storeys used as a manufactory of worsted'. There was a 20ft (6m) wheel with a (drying) kiln adjoining, from which the reasonable assumption can be made that some corn was then grown in Wensleydale.

The mill was not sold and two years later was largely destroyed by fire. Its shell was sold to local bankers who completed the 1853 rebuilding on a much larger scale, and it is this building that now adjoins the river, five storeys high and twice the size of the old structure. It continued its dual-purpose role, the spun yarn being distributed to hand-knitters in Wensleydale and Swaledale. The row of mill-workers' cottages by the roadside, and the longer row behind the mill building, probably date from the middle years of last century. Spinning seems to have ended in the 1870s, although corn-grinding continued. At the turn of the century the mill's third floor was used occasionally for social events such as dances, and in 1912 the building was adapted to become a flour-rolling mill. Yorkshire Farmers Ltd bought it in 1927 and the water-wheel was removed in 1937. Using modern machinery it continued operating as a flour-mill until 1959 when it became a store for animal feed, before changing hands in 1967, again being converted, this time into a coach and carriage museum. The whole complex of mill, mill-house and two rows of cottages form an interesting example of a small industrial hamlet in the Yorkshire Dales, and Yore Mill is the only surviving mill in Wensleydale which used the water of the river to provide its power. Other mills were built on tributary streams.

One other Wensleydale mill deserves a mention. Low Mill, on the north side of the green at Bainbridge, probably dates from around 1800, although according to Dr Arthur Raistrick, its plan, lay-out and machinery 'are still essentially seventeenth-century in character'. Low Mill was probably used throughout most of last century for grinding corn, and its brick-built drying kiln on the ground floor is an important feature of a recent restoration of the building. Corn-milling continued well into the present century, and although from 1920–9 the mill was also used as a dairy for the manufacture of Wensleydale cheese, milling – most likely of oats – went on until 1947 when flooding on the River Bain broke the dam and work ceased. Over the past few years much restoration has been carried out, and the 15ft (4.6m) internally breast-shot wheel has been repaired and can now be operated electrically. Low Mill is open on certain afternoons during the summer.

During the early years of the nineteenth century worsteds and knitting yarns continued to be made in Wensleydale, Swaledale and Dentdale, with important market outlets at Richmond, Barnard Castle and Kendal. Nidderdale concentrated on flax-spinning and the manufacture of hemp, but the valleys of the southern dales and Craven Pennines turned to cotton-spinning, which had become mechanised by 1780. For that area Skipton was the natural marketing outlet.

In Wharfedale, until Linton Mill on the south side of the river was demolished recently, it formed the dominant part of an interesting group of industrial buildings. Originally a manorial corn-mill it was rebuilt in the late eighteenth century as a worsted-mill, owned by the

Birkbecks, before turning to cotton-spinning. Around 1840 a small hamlet, now called Botany, was built to house the mill-workers. Textile manufacture declined; Linton Mill became a creamery, and then, in relatively recent years became a weaving-shed for the manufacture of cotton and rayon, finally closing in 1959. Farther down the river, Grassington Low Mill, on the site of an older water-powered corn-mill, saw the textile industry follow the sequence of worsted, cotton, silk, and flax-spinning during much of last century before eventually being saved from dereliction by conversion to residential use. The former millpond has been used for fish-farming for some years. Brow Well Fisheries concentrates on producing eggs, fry and fingerlings, with 2–3 million rainbow and brown trout from egg-size to 6in (15cm), these largest specimens weighing just over an ounce (28gm) and being fed three times daily. Fish are kept at Brow Mill for six to ten months before being transported to fish-farms in England, Wales and Scotland for further growing. The 'office' occupies a barn adjoining the pools, further proof of the fact that the best way to conserve old buildings is to find new uses for them.

Coal-mining

This was one of the oldest and longest surviving industries in the Dales. Coal occurs in a number of areas, usually near the base of the Millstone Grit and in the upper horizons of the Yoredales, locations high on the fells where a thin cover allowed mining to be carried out by sinking vertical shafts from the surface to the seams. Records show that a pit was worked near Tan Hill in 1296, and that in 1670 Lord Wharton leased it to three men conditionally on his being allowed to take, free of charge, 150 loads for his home at Wharton Hall near Kirkby Stephen. The important period of mining was during the eighteenth and nineteenth centuries, when coal was used for lime-burning, for lead-smelting in the new reverbatory furnaces and for domestic use before the railway allowed coal to be brought more cheaply into the Dales from Durham and South Yorkshire.

Evidence of old coal mines is most apparent in the spoil-heaps, usually of fine, blue-black shale, grassed over, frequently occurring in a line across a moor. These disc-shaped mounds, with a central depression, mark the bell-pits of shallow shafts (30–100ft/9–30m). The bell-pits were worked radially from the bottom of a shaft for a safe but limited distance. Then another shaft would be sunk along the seam, worked to safe limits as before, and subsequent shafts sunk. Bell-pits are linked by tracks and green lanes across the fells, along which the mined coal was carried by pack-horses to its places of use. Between Redmire and Reeth old pits are marked over a wide area of moors, and a concentrated network of associated tracks invites exploration on foot.

One of the most extensive areas of old coal-mines is on the high fells between the heads of Garsdale and Dentdale. Tracks from this led to the Galloway Gate, part of a very old drove road from Scotland to the big markets of the West Riding. Much of this is now a high-level surfaced road from Garsdale station to Dentdale, and a drive along it gives a good impression of the typical landscape of upland coal-mining. Coal from these pits was burned in houses in both these western dales until 1876, when the Settle–Carlisle railway brought cheaper and better coal to the district.

Collieries associated with Tan Hill are located in an area south and south-east of Tan Hill Inn. King's Pit Colliery (903065), reached by a green track over the moors, is known to have sent coal in the seventeenth century to some of the Wharton smelt mills in Swaledale and subsequently to the Old Gang Mills. William Gill Pits, about a mile to the east, has some ruined buildings – William Gill Houses – and some levels, with a good moorland track running eastwards along Annaside Edge to the Punchard Gill Levels at the eastern limit of the Tan Hill Coal.

A mile down the West Stonesdale road are the large spoil-heaps and ravaged ground around Moulds Gill Level with the ruins of the coal-store and a two-roomed building where customers waited in bad weather for coal to be brought out of the drift mine, as well as shelters for miners themselves (890054). Water stained a rust-brown colour flows from the former level of which the masonry entrance can just be identified. A photograph of c1910 shows a group of horses and carts at the Moulds Level, waiting to be loaded with coal for carriage into Keld and the upper Swaledale villages. During the 1926 General Strike, when Britain's main pits were silent, Tan Hill Colliery experienced a short-lived boom; miners worked as never before and there was a constant flow of coal-carts up and down Swaledale and Arkengarthdale, some of them coming even from Durham. A cart load of 6–7cwt (300–350kg) cost about 6s 8d (33p).

It is hard to realise now that, in 1851, four families lived at Tan Hill, comprising twenty-two men, women and children. Today, the rightful claim of the inn to be the highest pub in England, attracts hundreds of motorist visitors to these lonely heights. The inn is an equally important and welcoming point on the Pennine Way, whose route from the south passes close to a number of deep shafts, circular and lined with masonry, associated with coal-mining days.

The Pennine Way passes close to another extensive area of collieries, also on the Tan Hill Coal, some way to the south, on each side of the southern flanks of Great Shunner Fell from Cotterdale round to Fossdale near Hawes. Coal from these pits was used widely in Wensleydale well into the present century. Walkers on the Shunner Fell track above Hardraw will be readily aware of the many small bell-pits between Black Hill Moss and Bleak Haw, where beacons and 'piles of stones' near the route were almost certainly guides for coal-miners – bad-weather markers signifying where the pits were located. A track up the western side of Hearne Beck is still called the Hearne Coal Road. On the high fells of Abbotside Common between Wensleydale and Swaledale a number of small, isolated collieries provided coal for upland farms and limekilns in the eighteenth and nineteenth centuries. The Summer Lodge road from Askrigg over to Reeth passes at its highest point the area of Windgates Collieries, where bell-pits and shafts are visible close to the road on each side.

To the east, and at a lower level, the moors between Redmire and Grinton embrace the largest area of collieries in the Dales, covering 3 square miles of moorland between the two roads from Castle Bolton and Redmire which converge on Grinton. The Grinton Moor, Redmire Moor, Preston Moor and Bellerby Moor Collieries were all within the Bolton royalties, with coal being worked by lessees, the earliest lease being of 1569 for pits in Carperby township. In the following century large quantities of coal from many of the pits here were carried to the alum works at Guisborough, in Cleveland; leases were renewed at intervals until 1779 when they passed into the hands of lead-mine operators on Grassington Moor, where the coal was used in lead-ore smelting. Since Grassington is over 20 miles away it is evident, yet again, how much pack-horse traffic must have been constantly on the move throughout a large area of the Dales, most of it associated with coal-mining, lead-working, lime-burning and stone-quarrying.

Fleensop Colliery, on the long, lonely moorland ridge between Walden and Coverdale, has many shafts, levels and bell-pits, and generated its own network of tracks, as did the smaller group of pits on West Scrafton Moor between Coverdale and East Witton. However, one of the highest situated and most unusual collieries of the Dales was that on Fountains Fell, about 5 miles north-west of Malham. Crude documentation of these gives a fragmented picture of their working. Fountains Fell Colliery worked the same seams as the Tan Hill Colliery, from a few feet beneath the Millstone Grit cap of the summit (2,190ft/668m), to a depth of 160ft (49m). Calamine mines nearby may have encouraged surveyors and miners from the Burnley coalfield, and since coal was needed for calcining the calamine, a local source was preferable to that from Keighley, then in use. A borehole was sunk in 1807, although outcrop coal may have been used earlier. Deeper shafts were sunk from 1809, one man receiving 2s 6d (12½p) a day for 261 days' boring, another the same rate for 198 days' work. Some shafts were masonry-lined, necessitating carting suitable stone to the site, this in turn requiring improvement of existing pack-horse tracks, itself involving more stone. (The rate was 3s a day for the man and horse leading the stone.)

When the colliery was in production different jobs were involved. Miners entered hillside levels on the workable seams; coal was hauled up vertical shafts and sorted at the top (the two processes called banking), where coal was stored. A man loaded it on to the pack ponies (Galloways), and did other surface jobs; another man led the ponies away to the calamine works or to Malham. All this occurred at 2,000ft (600m) up on wind-swept fells. Except during severe weather 200–350 loads of coal would be produced and transported each week, each load being 2¼cwt, (115kg), giving an annual average of 8,000–11,000 loads, or 900–1,000 tons. Costs of production averaged 3s 6d (17½p) for a score of loads, with rates of pay for most men at 3s–3s 6d a day. Selling prices varied with the quality of coal, from 6½d to 1s per load.

Much of Fountains Fell coal proved to be too dirty for calcining (roasting) calamine, but it was found by experiment that the best-quality coal made a coke which was suitable, so in about 1812 a coke oven was built at the colliery – undoubtedly the highest-located coke oven in Britain – and coke from it was used in the calcining process. From 1815 coke was also used at the lead-smelting mill on Malham Moor. The remoteness of the Fountains Fell coke oven has helped to ensure its survival as a unique mining monument, 12ft (3.7m) square, igloo-shaped inside, with a low arch on its northern side. Pennine Way walkers, following their long-distance path a few hundred yards to the north, are its most likely visitors today, although the nearest road, Stainforth–Halton Gill, is only a mile away to the west.

Ingleton, more commonly associated with caves, waterfalls and Ingleborough, had a coalfield isolated not only from the main Yorkshire and Lancashire fields but also from the coal-seams beneath the high fells already described. Through the geological quirk of the Craven Fault, good seams of coal were found to exist 600–900ft (180–270m) below the surface, and by the middle of last century three deep workings had been established, at Newfield, Wilson Wood and Moorgarth. But by 1865 one had become worked out, one flooded and the third suffered from neglect. Ten years later they had been rejuvenated to the extent of employing 140 men, but by the end of the century had again declined.

However, in 1913 began the final flurry of coal-mining on the Ingleton field, when the New Colliery shafts were sunk to 900ft (270m). World War I saw the number of workers employed gradually rise and in 1917–20 about 500 men were employed there, the weekly coal production rising to 2,000 tons; an adult collier received 15s a week (75p). Coal was sold at 18s a ton (90p), but locals were allowed to fill a hand-cart for 2s (10p). Pit-head winding gear was of the double-wheel type familiar at many large collieries today, and six pit-ponies, accommodated in clean stables below ground, hauled tubs of coal from working faces to the bottom of the shaft.

When Ingleton New Colliery was opened, many miners came to work there from other northern coalfields, and were housed in New Village, known locally as the Model Village. The mine-owners contracted for the building of a hundred brick houses, each costing £91, with four bedrooms, living-room, parlour, scullery and pantry. Tenants paid, in the 1920s, 11s 8d (58p) a week for rates and rent. When New Colliery was closed down in 1937 tenants were given the chance of buying their houses. In the pits, machinery and equipment were left underground, and the shafts were sealed over. Trees now cover the slag-heaps near the former pit-head workings, and the two circles of colliery houses, with a green space in the middle, supplemented by a further twenty-six concrete houses built later by the company, all occupied, remain the largest industrial housing complex within the Yorkshire Dales.

Copper, Calamine and Brass

Although some evidence exists to suggest that copper-ore was mined on Pikedaw Hill (880638), above Malham, in the seventeenth century – probably from its carbonate ores, malachite (green) and azurite (blue) – no detailed account exists to indicate how it was obtained and worked. The ore is likely only to have been roasted to prepare it for the travelling ore-buyers who subsequently sold it to smelters, the smelting of copper-ore being a more technically complex process than could be accommodated locally. However, it is known that the copper mines were being worked in 1787–8, when miners at Pikedaw, seeking fresh sources of ore, broke through into a long, narrow, high natural cave which they named the Great Shake. In exploring its associated caverns they discovered deposits of calamine (zinc carbonate). In 1788 William Brayshaw, lessee of all mines on Malham Moor, applied to Thomas Lister of Gisburn, lord of the manor, for a lease to work the calamine deposits on Pikedaw Hill.

The mine was worked, with great difficulty, for about ten years. Several years then elapsed, when surveys were made to determine where to sink a shaft on to the best deposits. Additionally, a stream had to be diverted to reduce water problems in the workings. By 1807 improvements had been made, production of calamine increased, and the Pikedaw mine began almost twenty years of prosperous working.

Calamine, now called smithsonite, was not used as a source of pure metal, but was roasted in a process known as calcining. The resultant calcined calamine would then be added to granular copper, and the mixture would be heated in a special furnace for ten to twelve hours, to produce brass, an alloy of zinc and copper. Pikedaw calamine was merely calcined, the product then being sent to Cheadle, where the Cheadle Brass Company manufactured brass. The company was dissatisfied with Pikedaw calcining and advised how it could be improved, with the result that the calcining process was transferred from Pikedaw to Calamine House in the village of Malham, which has recently been restored and converted into a private house. Proper furnaces there made a far more satisfactory job of the calcining process.

Pack-ponies carried the calamine from Pikedaw to Malham, and the calcined calamine from Malham to Gargrave. Initially, the eastern part of the Leeds–Liverpool Canal was then used to transport it, via the Aire and Calder Navigation, to Gainsborough or Hull and subsequent shipment to London. From 1796, with the completion of the western part of the Leeds–Liverpool Canal over the summit as far as Burnley, transport to Cheadle used that route from Gargrave, the journey being completed by land carriage to Manchester and Cheadle.

Explorations for more calamine deposits over Malham Moor revealed sources of ochre, an oxide of iron widely used as a pigment combined with white lead and oil to make brown paint. Thomas Lister, by then Lord Ribblesdale, exploited the existence of ochre, and for a short while paint was produced at Malham. Calcined calamine was tried instead of lead as a base for paint, but with little success, and by 1830 customers for both calamine and ochre were obtaining the minerals from other sources, and the Malham Moor mines ceased working. Apart from a few spoil-heaps and the outlines of small reservoirs, surface remains of the Pikedaw copper and calamine workings are only a very meagre sign that, during thirty years of working life about 5,000 tons of calamine were produced there.

Lead-mining

No lead is mined in the Yorkshire Dales today. A century ago the picture was different, although even by then the industry was declining after reaching its peak between 1830 and 1850, with about 2,000 men working in the industry throughout the main mining areas in the Dales. All human activity associated with lead-mining has long since gone, but some miners have left records of their lives and work. Pioneering researches – subsequently written up and published – by Dr Arthur Raistrick, both in the field and from archival sources, throw an enormous amount of light on this most important industry. Additionally, many relics survive, particularly the stone buildings associated with the smelting process, and although rescue archaeology with the help of volunteer labour has stabilised some of these, a great deal has been lost through wilful neglect, vandalism, and the all-too-frequent appropriation of their good masonry by local landowners and farmers for their own purposes.

Veins of lead-bearing ore – galena (lead sulphide) – exist beneath the surface over an extensive area of the Dales (though not all inside the National Park), largely between 1,000ft (305m) and 2,000ft (610m). Mining and smelting were concentrated in two main areas: in the north, the ore-field embraced Arkengarthdale, Swaledale and the northern side of Wensleydale; the southern field extended in a belt of land a few miles wide from Buckden in Wharfedale to Pateley Bridge in Nidderdale. The galena veins occur in the rocks of the Lower Carboniferous Series, originating millions of years ago as hot gases or liquids being forced from deep in the earth into fissures and joints in surface rocks, mainly limestone, and to a much lesser extent, sandstone. Most veins of ore in the north Pennine field lie vertically, like upturned table-tops, from a few inches to 2–3ft (60–90cm) thick, as continuous or intermittent ribbons only a few yards long, sometimes up to 6 miles long, and occasionally found with horizontal side-branches called flats, sometimes pipes. Mining was always very uncertain, for the extent and quality of a vein was never known until it was explored and worked. However, knowledge gained through experience did show that flats usually produced higher-grade ore, veins were often parallel to one another and, being vertical, could be followed up or down.

It is thought that the Romans mined lead, at Hurst in Swaledale and on Greenhow Hill. Monasteries within and beyond the Dales held mining rights on their estates, and lead-ore was certainly mined during medieval times. But the main period of activity was between 1790 and 1860, and most of what can be seen today is from that period. Early mining of veins near the surface was by the bell-pit method also used for coal-mining, and examples of old bell-pit workings, identified by the circular spoil-heaps following the line of a vein, can be seen on Lea Green (996656) north of Grassington, and on Grinton Moor (035961). On Greenhow Hill (110646) the Jackass Level is one of the best examples of an old working driven horizontally into the hillside, probably of seventeenth-century date. Its mouth, less than 2ft (60cm) wide and 5ft (1.5m) high has obviously been hewn by picks from a gritstone outcrop, a few hundred yards from the remains of the early-nineteenth-century Cockhill smelt mill.

Before any ore veins could be worked they had to be located. In the northern ore-field the principal veins lie approximately east–west and are thus cut by the tributary valleys which feed into Swaledale from the north. Occasionally veins came near to the surface, giving early prospectors relatively few excavation problems, but to help location a system known as 'hushing' was used. This involved scouring by water. On the crest of a hill above a suspected vein a turf dam, sometimes strengthened with stones, would be constructed across a moorland stream, impounding its waters into a reservoir. When sufficient had accumulated, the dam was broken, and the released water surged down the hillside, scouring away vegetation, soil and loose rocks, and exposing the underlying rock which, it was hoped, contained veins of ore. Loose ore would be swept to the valley bottom to be recovered and worked, and if a vein was revealed a level would be driven into the hillside along it. The first few yards of such a level, or adit, passing through soft ground, would be arched with masonry, as was the level mouth; scores of such openings can be identified over much of the northern ore-field. Adits were driven with a slight upward incline which would help to drain the ever-present water away from working faces, and most were laid with narrow-gauge railway lines along which tubs of ore could be removed, either by pony-power or man-power.

By the late eighteenth and early nineteenth centuries most of the upper veins had become worked out. Mining companies, usually formed by local landowners and merchants, were then the only sources of such capital as was needed to finance exploration at deeper levels by driving longer adits from lower parts of valleys to reach the ore-bearing zones. Access levels through 'dead' or barren ground were expensive and slow to drive. The Sir Francis Level in Gunnerside Gill, for example, begun in 1864, cost £10 a fathom (6ft/1.8m) for the first 202 fathoms, and took five years. Rock-drills powered by an air-compressor speeded up progress, but the introduction of dynamite in 1873 made the biggest improvement, so that the next 550 fathoms were driven in a third of the time and at only half the cost of manual work.

Deadmen, or sappers, drove the levels and dug the shafts. Pickmen, using picks, hammers and oak wedges to crack the rock, and then wielding shovels, worked the vein. They were also armed with candles, clay (to stand them in) and matches. Both groups worked in small teams or partnerships; excavated ore brought to the surface was taken to the 'bousesteads', or 'bouse teams', which were series of walled bays in which each partnership's ore was initially dressed. Pay was for the lead-ore yield from a particular group's bouse – the mixture of ore and waste rock – and was for a bing of ore of smeltable quality, a bing being 8cwt (400kg).

From the bousesteads the ore went to the dressing-floor to be crushed, separated and cleaned. Good examples of bousesteads can be seen in Gunnerside Gill (944955) and Old Gang (975006), while recently restored ones at Beldi Hill, near Keld (904007), on private ground, can be visited by prior arrangement with the National Park Office at Bainbridge. There are other examples, in poorer condition, above Woodhall, in Wensleydale (983903), and in Cogden Gill south of Grinton (046963).

Ore-dressing involved the breaking down of bouse and the removal of as much impurity as possible, to produce a concentrate of almost pure galena. Picking over by hand and then breaking by a bucker (a hammer with a flat, iron plate as head), or by a roller-crusher powered by a water-wheel, aimed to produce pieces 2–10mm in size. To separate ore from gangue (parent rock) water was used; in an ore-gangue mixture of gravel-sized fragments, a shaking sieve in a barrel of water brings the heavier galena to the bottom, the lighter gangue to the top. The hotching-tub, or jigger, worked by levers, was an application of this method. Finer material of sand-sized particles was better dealt with in a buddle or sluice, allowing water to run over the ore-gangue mixture contained in an open, slightly sloping surface. A restored circular buddle can be seen at Beldi, in Swaledale.

Water was used in all these operations, either to power water-wheels or for ore-separation. Thus, dressing-floors with their heaps of fine-grained spoil are usually near streams from which, at points higher up their courses, specially constructed water-courses, or launders, directed a supply to where it was needed. Grassington Moor shows a maze of water-courses, fed from a reservoir high up the moor and linking a series of dressing-floors. Indeed, the Duke's High and Low Watercourses (named after the Duke of Devonshire, owner of the Grassington Moor mines), started during the last quarter of the eighteenth century, extend a total of 6½ miles, using water collected at Priest Tarn (1,680ft/ 512m). At the height of mining operations in 1850, the combined water-courses had acquired nine dams for storage and regulation reservoirs, and powered eight large water-wheels, three for winding and pumping at shafts, five for crushing and dressing the ore.

Also on Grassington Moor are a number of circular gin-races – areas of grass or gravel worn flat by horses harnessed to a wooden frame and windlass device, which raised or lowered large iron buckets called 'kibbles' in the deep mine-shafts. Buckets of water were also hauled up to help drain the mine, a continuous process needing at least six horses working in pairs for three hours at a stretch. In the mines water was the miner's enemy; at the dressing-floors and at the smelt mills it was his ally.

Most lead-smelting mills used the ore-hearth, which evolved from the small blast-furnace, and which could be cheaply and quickly built. It operated for one or two shifts, smelting about a ton of lead during each shift, and was thus suited to the small partnerships characteristic of the Dales. The ore-hearth, similar to a blacksmith's hearth, was usually 4–5ft (1.2–1.5m) square and placed beneath a masonry arch spanning 12–15ft (3.6–4.5m) and 6–8ft (1.8–2.4m) in depth, which allowed working space at the sides and front. Behind the ore-hearth was a bellows-room, where water-powered bellows drove air through openings called 'tuyères' into the hearth.

The cast-iron hearth, about 2ft (60cm) square and 1ft (30cm) deep, with an integral, projecting grooved 'workstone' sloping from one side, was supported in strongly built masonry. Using coal or peat as fuel, ore was heated in a current of air; its impurities burned off as gases, and the residual metal was initially run off into pre-heated cast-iron sumpter-pots and subsequently 'tapped' into pigs of lead of about 1¼cwt (60kg) each.

Larger, reverbatory furnaces came into use about 1700 and were up to 18ft (5.5m) long, 12ft (3.6m) wide and 10ft (3m) high, usually built by lead-smelting companies.

Initially, most mills had short flues to carry away the poisonous fumes

Mill ruins at Blakethwaite Smelt Mill at the head of Gunnerside Gill, Swaledale. The mill was built in 1820; the arched building beyond was the peat-store

caused by the smelting process, but from the early years of last century these were replaced by long flues, either horizontal (as on Grassington Moor) or slanting up a hillside, as at Grinton, Old Gang, Gunnerside and Langthwaite. These long flues culminated at a terminal stack, of which those at Grassington and Malham have been restored, and the ones at Grinton, Cobscar and Old Gang are sufficiently in evidence to be recognisable, while the rest have largely collapsed. Valuable lead deposits accumulated on the inner walls of flues, which were periodically scraped, and the sublimed lead was re-smelted. The arched masonry of many lengths of flue has survived remarkably well, and if you are prepared to stoop you can explore some of the flues on Grassington Moor, above Grinton, and in Arkengarthdale.

Colourful Settle market on a Tuesday morning, from the steps of the Shambles. The 'Royal Oak' beyond is a seventeenth-century structure with eighteenth-century buildings adjoining. The busy A65 Skipton-Kendal road passes the western side of Market Place

Great Octagon Mill CB, built c1804, photographed in 1949, now completely demolished. High Eskeleth can be seen on the hillside beyond

Probably the most evocative lead-mining landscapes in the Dales are on the Swaledale–Arkengarthdale mining field. Both Gunnerside Gill and the Old Gang complex to its north-east reveal the ravaged scenery of lead-mining days, while on the moors above Arkengarthdale scenes of desolation extend over a vast area. It is not surprising that some of the most popular guided walks in the National Park's summer programme take visitors to the heart of these areas.

Gunnerside Gill, in particular, has a haunting if melancholy beauty to reward the walker prepared to explore the steep-sided valley for 2 or 3 miles. Its upper part is riven by hillside gashes produced by repeated hushings, with fans of scree and rock debris at the foot of steep slopes. Easily identified are the dark mouths of old levels, adits and drainage tunnels, as well as the remains of stores, mine shops, stables, a peat store and smelt mills. Most of the remains here and in Old Gang date from the busy years of last century, roughly 1830–70, and are contem-

View down upper Swaledale from above Thwaite. The barn (storing hay for winter feed) and the walled fields are typical of Swaledale. Note the Swaledale sheep

porary with the impressive Grinton Smelt Mill, in the valley of the
Cogden Beck, on the moors about a mile south of Grinton village, easily accessible from the Leyburn road. This is the only smelt mill still
roofed, and although its interior has been largely gutted and used for
other purposes, sufficient survives to allow an impression of what the
process involved. Unhappily, Arkengarthdale's greatest architectural
glory, the great Octagon Mill of c1806, has vanished; its arched walls
survived until the 1960s, but its timber-framed roof was dismantled earlier. In a field near-by, easily seen from the road, its contemporary but
smaller powder house, also octagonal, is still roofed, an elegantly functional building which illustrates the fine quality of masonry characteristic of industrial buildings in the Dales.

The Arkengarthdale mines were acquired by a Dr Bathurst in 1656
and were subsequently developed by his grandson, Charles, whose initials CB in the company name are perpetuated not only in the name of
the local inn, but also in the community – surely the only place in
Britain named by initials! By the eighteenth century many mines and
mills were on the estates of large landowners. The Denys family took
over the Wharton estates and mines in Swaledale; the London
(Quaker) Lead Company acquired those at Marrick and Grinton, and
leased others in Wensleydale, where the principal mill was Keld Heads,
near Preston-under-Scar, just outside the Park boundary. On the hills
above, the terminal stack of the extensive system of flues is a prominent
skyline accent, but nearby Cobscar Mill is largely ruinous, and the
mines reservoir is a reedy haunt of black-headed gulls.

Mining prosperity was invariably related to the world price of lead.
Big fluctuations resulted in boom times alternating with slumps. One
such depression, in 1829–33, forced many small mines to close, with
wages falling to 8s a week. Companies could usually ride out these lean
periods, and were able to continue until the 1880s. By then, many of
the richer veins were exhausted, and the poorer ones were too costly to
work. A few isolated mines continued until about 1910, but for three-
quarters of a century no appreciable amounts of lead-ore have been
mined in the area, and all the old miners have died. Old spoil-heaps
have been reworked for fluorite and barytes, usually only on a small
scale, and yields have been less than in Weardale or the Peak District.
Relics, tools and equipment have gone to local museums at Skipton,
Grassington, Pateley Bridge, Hawes and Reeth, but a great opportunity
has been lost to turn, say, Grassington, Gunnerside or Old Gang into
an imaginative museum of lead-mining.

However, the Yorkshire novelist, Thomas Armstrong, used

Old Powder-house CB, built c1804

Coke oven, c1810, on the summit plateau of Fountains Fell, near Malham

nineteenth-century lead-mining in Swaledale as the theme for his fine novel, *Adam Brunskill*. It vividly evokes the hard life of the lead-miners, and their firm belief that the next vein of ore would be the best. In the story we meet also 't'owd man', that integral part of Dales mining history, which seems to be all things to all miners, a generic term for anything to do with the job, but especially for the spirits of miners who have gone before. In an autumnal dusk, with a wind moaning around ruined buildings amid the lonely moors, it is not difficult to sense an echo of their presence.

Quarrying

Reference has been made (Chapter 1) to the small parish and township quarries from which stone for local buildings was obtained. Scars of small-scale, long-abandoned quarries have become grassed over, or are clothed with trees and vegetation. Some have been used as official local authority tips, others are less officially used in this way. Few, if any, written records about them survive. However, some later quarries have been researched, especially those in upper Wensleydale around Hawes. These are unusual in not having exposed quarry faces, since the stone was mined underground. Within the Yoredale Series of rocks in Wensleydale, names have been given to the various limestone strata. The sandstones which occur, about 1,150ft (350m), between the Simonstone and Middle Limestones were found to be very flaggy, coarse grained and relatively soft, and being well layered could be raised and split without great difficulty.

Above Burtersett and Gayle this layer of Burtersett flags was worked extensively from about 1860 to 1930, with a production peak during the last decade of the nineteenth century. The beds were worked inwards, from hillsides. Underground, while main galleries ran for about 450yd (400m), lateral, secondary workings extended in many directions and were always subject to collapse. The 'pillar and post' method was used, with solid stone pillars left in some places to support the roof, piles of waste stone – 'backfill' – in others, supplemented by timber props called 'puncheons'. Occasionally, lengths of old iron rail served this purpose. In his well-researched booklet, *Burtersett Quarries*, David Hall records the methods of obtaining the stone, in which teams of six men, working in two groups of three, tackled each working face. Huge hewn blocks were finally removed by horse-drawn, four-wheeled bogeys, 27½in gauge.

The sites of the workings are identified by big heaps of waste stone

adjoining the flat dressing-floors near the entrances to the levels –
openings of arched masonry. Remains of sheds and loading-bays can be
seen, together with the meagre ruins of a blacksmith's shop. When the
quarries at Burtersett and Gayle were busy, three or four large waggon-
loads, horse-drawn, were taken down to Hawes station each day.
Bulmer's Directory for 1890 records 15,000 tons of stone passing
through Hawes in one year, much of it said to have been sent to Lancashire mill towns. Locally, the stone was used for building some houses
in Hawes and sixteen quarrymen's cottages in Burtersett, as well as
being used for many roofs of barns and farms in the area. But perhaps
the most enduring reminders of these quarries are not the houses but
the stone-flagged paths or causeways used by quarrymen at Hawes,
Gayle, Hardraw and Burtersett, laid down by quarry-owners to protect
the meadow land from wear and tear by quarrymen's boots as they
walked to and from their dark, unpleasant work.

Marble

Some of the limestones in the Yoredale Series are hard enough to take a
polish. One of these which is black, and another more grey in shade,
were suitable for ornamental use and were worked as Dent marble. On
steep hillsides in Dentdale and Garsdale, especially in the gills, thin
seams of these limestones were exposed, and were worked for over a
century after their discovery in about 1760. Within the following fifty
years the marble industry had become organised, so that by 1810 the
water-wheel of High Mill, in Arten Gill, changed from driving mill
machinery to operating marble-cutting saws. Lower down the gill Low
Mill was constructed as a polishing mill and soon added cutting equipment. Its wheelpit can be identified among overgrown masonry by the
roadside above the narrow-waisted Stone House bridge in upper
Dentdale (772858). By 1830 trade had expanded, with many men
employed at the quarries and mills, and Dent marble was being used,
mainly for fireplaces and floors, not only locally, but as far afield as
Newcastle, Liverpool and London. Carriers had to transport the product, by pack-horse trains, to Gargrave, where the Leeds–Liverpool
Canal offered a convenient route to distant places. The arrival of the
railway in 1876 stimulated the industry, but this boost was soon cancel-
led out by the imports of cheaper Italian marble at about the same time,
some of this even being sent by rail to Dent for cutting and polishing,
though not sufficient to maintain a buoyant trade. The local industry
slowly declined, and all working ceased about 1900.

There is an interesting footnote to the story. Although High Mill has completely vanished, a young visitor, William Armstrong, was fishing in Arten Gill in 1835, and became intrigued by the highly inefficient water-wheel in its picturesque setting. It encouraged him to take up the study, first of water power, subsequently of steam and then electrical power, which led, later in the century, to the development of the huge Armstrong empire of heavy industry on Tyneside. The Arten Gill viaduct, high above Stone House and the pack-horse road beneath, is built of rock-faced blocks of Dent marble – a rare use of an ornamental stone, probably justified only on the grounds of convenient quarrying nearby.

Lime-burning

During his 1770 tour Arthur Young commented, 'upon the black moorland soils the use [of lime] is exceedingly great'. By then a start had been made on enclosing land on the moor edge. After walling, enclosed land was burned to remove rough heather, sedge and sometimes bracken. Then it was drained, followed by the addition of lime to sweeten the sour soil in the hope of making usable pasture. Young recorded his observations in Langstrothdale, but recent coniferous plantations now clothe the rough pastures between High and Low Greenfield where he noted experiments carried out in 1774 by a farmer using the methods described. The land was then sown with turnips, followed by a mixture of rye-grass, clover and hay seed. Thus, extensive walling and grazing improved 200 acres (80ha) of former rough pasture, and on a subsequent visit Young noticed that the enclosed land was stocked with 20 horses, 40 cows and 1,200 sheep, while 300 young stock grazed summer pasture on the adjoining fells. Throughout the following fifty years similar improvements to marginal land were changing the farming pattern, and the prosperity of the Dales.

Enormous amounts of lime were needed. Of limestone there was no shortage, but in order to convert this into lime, kilns were required. These survive in their hundreds throughout the area, easily recognised by their black, cave-like mouths at the front of small, turret-like structures, occasionally seen near a road, as above Keld in Swaledale, near Appersett, and elsewhere in Wensleydale and Wharfedale, but more usually hidden away near convenient limestone outcrops, by upland tracks, and more likely to be visited by walkers.

There was a time when almost every Dales farm had its own kiln, or one was shared by perhaps two or three farms. However, there were some larger 'selling' kilns which were worked on a commercial basis. One of these, close to the road under Knipe Scar near Kettlewell, was recently restored under the auspices of the National Park Committee and the Trust Lords of Kettlewell, owners of the kiln. Local craftsmen, supported by National Park Conservation Volunteers, carried out the work. A public footpath through Knipe Wood passes close to the kiln, allowing a view of one of the humbler, but most characteristic, features of the Dales landscape.

Kilns were usually built into a hillside, preferably near to the base of a limestone outcrop, so that quarried stone, broken into small lumps, could be tipped straight into the bowl – a funnel-shaped lining of sandstone, its top few feet cylindrical, tapering to a neck at the bottom, below which is a grate for collecting the burnt lime and ash. The bowl is

Running or field kiln at Chapel-le-Dale, with Ingleborough in snow beyond

contained within a squat tower of dry-stone masonry, limestone or sandstone, squarish or slightly bow-fronted, 15–20ft (4.5–6m) across and about the same height. The front has a recessed hearth from which the accumulated lime and ash can be raked out. In use, a kiln was charged with alternate layers of quarried limestone and fuel – usually coal, which was ideally and commonly obtained from coal-pits higher up the fells. One part of coal with four parts of limestone gave a suitable mixture for burning, and as the mixture slowly burned through, emitting clouds of smoke and fumes in the process, it could be kept charged with more limestone and fuel. Even a small field kiln might thus burn for two or three days, a 'selling' kiln for a week or more. A few days' firing could yield 300 horse-loads of lime, each of 2½cwt (130kg), for a farmer's own use or for selling at 4d (2p) a load. Four loads made a cartful, and ten carts was sufficient for an acre of land.

Dales limekilns saw a century of use, roughly from 1750 to 1850, or even a few years later, when plumes of fire and smoke streamed into the sky and the red glow of kilns at night was a common sight. Although most of the lime was used to sweeten moorland soils, some was used as the base for lime mortar in the construction of farmhouses, barns and cottages that were built during those busy years. Now, the kilns are silent, their profiles easily recognised, but many have become derelict and broken, convenient dumps for a variety of rubbish.

6
EXPLORING THE MARKET TOWNS

The physical structure of the Yorkshire Dales is such that no single town can claim to be its 'capital'. Even the administration of the National Park is shared by two offices, at Grassington and Bainbridge, in Wharfedale and Wensleydale respectively. Each major valley is served by a market town: Swaledale looks to Richmond, Wensleydale to Leyburn, Wharfedale to Skipton, Ribblesdale to Settle, and the western dales to Sedbergh. Additionally, and largely as a result of improved communications arising from the turnpike roads of the second half of the eighteenth century, Hawes, in upper Wensleydale became increasingly important as a market centre serving the upper valleys of Swaledale, Wensleydale, Ribblesdale and the western dales, and, to some extent, Wharfedale above Kettlewell. A wider view would include Ilkley, Ripon, Kirkby Stephen, Kirkby Lonsdale, Masham, Pateley Bridge and Bentham, all outside the Park area. Of these, only Ilkley and Pateley Bridge are to be considered here.

Ilkley

In age and size Ilkley comes first. On the moors to its south, Bronze Age and Iron Age settlers have left their marks, mainly in the form of carved stones, of which the 'Swastika' stone, still an enigma for archaeologists, is best known. The Romans knew Ilkley as Olicana and established an important fort by the river's south bank near the present parish church, whose tower includes two Roman altars built into its base. In the churchyard itself three Anglo-Saxon crosses survive from the ninth-century Anglian settlement and nearby the former six-teenth-century manor-house now houses a folk museum. In Church Street and Bridge Street eighteenth-century houses provide additional links in the continuity of Ilkley's long history.

That same century saw the discovery, close to the house called White Wells on Ilkley Moor, of a cold spring whose water was found to have curative properties. The building became the nascent centre from which developed Ilkley's fame as a spa. After Dr Granville had visited it in the 1830s during his tour of English spas, he described Ilkley as a 'primitive and simple village . . . a rural retreat', albeit with some com-fortable lodging houses. By then, those in the upper echelons of factory society in the busy industrial West Riding would almost certainly have known Ilkley and would probably have stayed there for a few weeks in the summer. But the place was unknown outside Yorkshire and Lancashire.

The railway reached Ilkley in 1865 and changed that, but not before two great 'hydropathic establishments' – 'hydros' for short – had been built. In 1860 Cuthbert Brodrick, responsible for Leeds Town Hall, de-signed the Italianate Wells House, now a teachers' training college. East of the town a former mayor of Leeds built in 1844 a turreted, battlemented hydro as pseudo-Scottish as its ridiculous name, Ben Rhydding, a linguistic affront to its site on the slopes of Rombald's Moor which had previously been a field bearing the name Beau Rid-ding. A community grew up round the site, with a station added later, and between the wars the hydro became the Golf Hotel. During World War II it was acquired by the Wool Secretariat, and at the end of the war it was demolished, probably a merciful release. The railways un-doubtedly made Ilkley into a successful spa, and its tree-lined avenues and promenades evoke to a delightful degree its late Victorian and Edwardian dignified opulence.

Like many North country boys of my generation I spent many holi-days at Ilkley during the 1930s, when one of the traditional walks was across Rombald's Moor to Dick Hudson's. It seemed so spacious up there compared with the streets of Ilkley itself, and the gritty, sandy, well-trodden track probably impressed itself on my memory, for I still enjoy, of all types of walking, that which takes me across similar moor-land tracks, rough textured and stony among the August heather. The hard-earned ham-and-eggs teas at Dick Hudson's were undoubted highlights of holiday weeks in apartments. Happily, there are still places in the Dales where such traditional meals are served, and I still believe that to be really enjoyed they must be earned by at least an afternoon's good walk and preferably a whole day's one. Ilkley's Cow and Calf rocks induced a different thrill. On the famous gritstone outcrop there was the sensuous satisfaction of rock beneath the hands and fingers, the thrill of conquest, the joy of being apparently on top of a little world. Scenery as such means little to the child at the time but must imprint itself on the mind to become part of experience. Fifty years have not diminished my delight in crags, cliffs and limestone scars. For me, and probably for thousands of others, Ilkley and its moors were the seed-bed of a lifetime's joy of walking in the Dales.

Skipton

Originally called Sceptone by Anglian sheep-farmers who had settled there, this southern gateway to the Dales was chosen by the Norman Robert de Romille as site for his castle, which he built on a well-protected rock above the Ellerbeck gorge. He soon established a market, and in 1203 the granting of a three-day fair at Trinity brought more trade, and more importance. A weekly market in medieval times dealt in perishable goods and was a local affair attended by the small buyers and sellers – the same is to a large extent true of the market today. A fair was a bigger event, still relatively local, involving bigger quantities of goods, including many of a less perishable nature – metal, fabric, leather, salt, spices and wines. Some items at fairs were seasonal, such as wool and cattle, and the time of a fair was chosen to suit the particular locality. Over the years, fairs within the same area were arranged to take place consecutively so that merchants from a distance could attend more than one. From the thirteenth to the eighteenth centuries a district with good seasonal fairs and weekly markets was virtually self-supporting.

Skipton was the centre of such a district. The backbone of its present shape, the High Street, had been established down the hill between the castle at the top and the line of a Roman road at the bottom by the fourteenth century. A weekly market concentrated on corn, and by 1756 the number of fairs had grown to a dozen. The town's arable fields were then being enclosed, and a resultant move towards livestock caused a decline in Skipton's corn trade. Stock-rearing farmers required large quantities of corn for their animals, and as most of this was now grown elsewhere a market for it became necessary. The present Newmarket Street marks where this developed.

Advances and changes in building styles start at the top of the social

scale and gradually spread downwards. After the Civil War the redoubtable Lady Anne Clifford on inheriting her estates started a rebuilding programme. Skipton Castle was restored and extended, and
property-owners along the High Street, following Lady Anne's example, built new houses for themselves using local stone. In the 1720s
woolcombers and weavers were allowed to build houses at the bottom
end of the town. In the middle of the century the Keighley–Kendal
turnpike was built, passing through the town and emphasising its importance as the collecting centre for wool produced on the Craven
uplands, leaving Malham Moor Fair to concentrate on livestock, particularly Highland cattle brought south by Scottish drovers.

In 1774 the Yorkshire section of the Leeds–Liverpool Canal was
completed, so Skipton was linked to flourishing industrial areas on both
sides of the Pennines. More trade ensued, mainly in limestone, fertilisers and food. By the end of the century Skipton, more than any other
town in or near the National Park, was being drawn into the Industrial
Revolution. The worsted cloth industry became firmly established, and
in the early nineteenth century new mills were built along the canal
banks, taking advantage of the convenience of using barge-carried coal

Skipton parish church, mainly fifteenth century, at the top of High Street. It
shows the typical profile of Dales churches – long and low, with no division
between nave and chancel

to power the steam engines driving their machinery. Mills needed labour; more houses, shops and schools were required, and between 1801 and 1831 Skipton's population more than doubled, to 4,800; it then stayed constant for twenty years. Evidence of this increase can be seen in the long, narrow yards running off High Street, especially on its western side. Most of them date from the 1830s, surviving as narrow openings between present-day shops and leading to alleyways and terraces of stone houses, those on one side of a yard facing the backs of houses in the next yard.

Between 1850 and 1880 cotton-spinning mills were added to Skipton's other industrial buildings, with another housing upsurge, this time mainly in the form of terraces of sturdily built stone houses on the south-eastern slopes above the canal. The population again more than doubled, between 1871 and 1911, from 6,000 to 13,000, a figure which then stabilised. Now, some of Skipton's early Victorian housing has gone, and many new housing estates have been added to the town's edges. Although Saturday is the official market day, stalls add colour and vitality to High Street almost every day of the week. Every Monday sees a cattle market, and Skipton's position on the trans-Pennine A59, as well as on the equally busy A65 which links West Yorkshire with the Lake District along the line of the Keighley–Kendal turnpike, adds to its commercial and industrial prosperity. It is also the administrative centre for the Craven District Council.

Richmond

At the opposite corner of the area Richmond, administrative centre of the Richmondshire District Council, is the northern gateway to the National Park. More than that, it is one of England's most splendid historic castle-towns, comparable perhaps only to Ludlow in Shropshire. Unfortunately, recent, ill-planned expansion up the hillside to its north has forever marred the fine backcloth to the prospect from the castle keep, but the heart of the town still shows its medieval plan, centred on the Norman castle and its outer bailey.

The best way to explore Richmond is by starting at the castle, where Scolland's Hall is one of the oldest halls in existence, and the twelfth-century gate-house keep, at over 90ft (27m) is one of the highest. The bird's-eye view from this reveals the medieval street plan, with wynds, passages and streets radiating from the perimeter of the market place. Finkle Street, one of a number of medieval streets, leads through to Newbiggin, 'new' in the late twelfth century, and now, with its cobbles, trees and Georgian frontages, Richmond's most elegant thoroughfare. Frenchgate, originally the main way into the town from the north-east, now closed to through traffic, is lined with elegant houses illustrating Richmond's social, administrative and commercial importance in the eighteenth century. There, and throughout the town, details in doorways and windows, textural contrasts of stone and brick, delight the eye, with all buildings in small-town scale, apart from the castle which always dominates. To its west, New Road represents an eighteenth-century improved access to John Carr's Green Bridge which replaced a medieval structure and carried the Richmond–Lancaster turnpike away to the south–west. A town walk should include Castle Walk, terraced high above the river, beneath the towering outer walls of the castle bailey. Westwards is the wooded lower valley of Swaledale, and from above Cornforth Hill the view is enhanced by Culloden Tower's distinctive shape.

Richmond's parish church of St Mary stands, unusually, outside the town walls. Holy Trinity, islanded in the market place and now housing the Green Howards' Regimental Museum, was never more than a chapel. The town's only other medieval building is Grey Friars' Tower, the fifteenth-century sole survival of an earlier Franciscan foundation. In Richmond's townscape it performs the visual function of an important church tower. Nearby is one of the town's greatest treasures, the Royal Georgian Theatre of 1788, restored to theatrical use in 1963. Its tiny auditorium seats 240 people, many of whom occupy the original seats and boxes in one of the country's oldest theatre buildings.

Settle

When the boundaries of the National Park were drawn, Settle – like Richmond – was just excluded. Situated at an important river crossing on an historic trade route between Cumbria and West Yorkshire, where the Ribble leaves its upper valley and flows through a softer landscape before swinging westwards into Lancashire, it acquired a market charter in 1249. On the frontier between livestock farming of the uplands to its north and the arable farming of the middle reaches of the Ribble valley to the south, it was bound to succeed as a market and trading centre. Market day is Tuesday, when the market place is crammed with colourful stalls, with the unusual two-storey Shambles an attractive focal point. The arcaded arches of its ground floor are probably eighteenth

Richmond Castle, the great Norman keep from the south-east

century, but the cottages above were a nineteenth-century addition. The market stalls display a wide range of goods: apart from the vegetables, fruit, meat and fish, you can expect to find much locally made craftwork, woollen goods, produce and preserves, while the shops around the market place, almost all small, independent, family-owned concerns, admirably complement these items.

Like many other small market towns Settle has a family atmosphere, the result of remaining compact and intimate, and of being reasonably faithful to its past. There has been no large-scale destruction of old buildings, and the town happily retains many late-seventeenth-century houses together with a large number of buildings from the late eighteenth century onwards when the town experienced a surge in growth as local industries developed, thus making Settle less dependent on its agricultural hinterlands. In 1753 the Keighley–Kendal road became a turnpike, with the aim of improving communications between the important wool-producing areas of Westmorland and the increasingly important markets at Skipton and Halifax. Settle lay on the new road, which changed the town's whole orientation and subsequently brought great developments. The old road from the east had come over the moors from Long Preston, by Hunter Bark, entering the town by Settle Green with its village appearance and old stone cottages. The new approach, now followed by the A65, along a lower level, quickly entered the market place before turning left into Kirkgate and then northwards to the bridge. This winding route from the market place was, in 1804, changed for the more direct route along Church Street.

The turnpike brought prosperity for the inns, some of which moved their locations to take advantage of the passing traffic. A walk around the town with the aid of the Civic Society's leaflet, *Settle Town Trail*, highlights the many interesting buildings, the squares, yards, small houses and workshops, huddling beneath Castlebergh's frowning limestone outcrop. By following the various streets from the market place – Cheapside, Kirkgate, Constitution Hill, Castle Hill, Victoria Street, Albert Street and Station Road – you will be rewarded by many surprises, including decorative doorways and elaborate date panels, mainly of the seventeenth century. Settle's outstanding building is undoubtedly The Folly, dating from 1675, a 'capricious extravaganza of windows and splendidly carved masonry', now an antiques showroom. Unmistakably Tudor in appearance, it is completely out of local character but nonetheless attractive.

It was from a century later that a rapid growth in Settle's population, and the resultant demand for houses, brought about many of the yards

'The Folly', Settle, built by Richard Preston in 1675–9

which were developed behind existing buildings on street frontages. Talbot Yard in the High Street was one of the earliest, and was built for the inn as a courtyard away from the High Street. Among its features are a timber-supported flat roof behind the entrance arch; and stone steps leading to a tiny cottage above the arch. When Edward Dayes visited the town in 1803 he wrote, 'In Settle many of the houses about the market place have their ascent to the upper storey on the outside.'

Commercial Yard, built originally for the Commercial Hotel in 1774, is long and narrow with buildings along both sides, and a second smaller yard beyond, where coaches could be turned and horses changed. Land was in short supply at the time when Settle's population was increasing so that it was usual practice to squash houses and cottages in the crofts and gardens behind roadside buildings, adding to existing buildings and even building upwards. The resulting piecemeal growth was unplanned and uneven, but gradually each yard acquired its own distinction and name, usually that of the owner or builder, surviving today as Tatham's Yard, Radcliffe's Yard, Twistleton's Yard and Howson's Yard. Sometimes, as in Chapel Square, the arched entrance gave way to a more open one and although changes have occurred it still retains a pleasantly quiet atmosphere.

In common with other market towns Settle had a wide range of traders, as the early Baines' directories testify. The 1821 edition refers to dressmakers, boot and shoe makers, tailors, cotton-spinners, plumbers and glaziers, joiners, plasterers, blacksmiths and whitesmiths, corn millers, saddlers, ropemakers, millwrights, tanners, butchers, tea-dealers, tallow chandlers and clockmakers. By the river, at the end of Kirkgate, Procter's Mill (now King's Mill) changed from corn to cotton, enlarged its premises and built cottages – Procter's Row – for employees in 1833. Nearby was the old crossing of the Ribble at Kendalmans' Ford, a name commemorated in a new housing development in Giggleswick across the river.

Settle's secret corners are worth seeking out. Perhaps the most appealing part of the town is above High Way, towards Upper Settle and the Green. An old milestone near the primary school records distances to London, Kirkby Lonsdale, Hawes, Skipton and Lancaster. Beyond it, Albert Hill – narrow, with signs of cobbles – climbs to the Green, and there was no further expansion of the town in Victorian times in that direction because of steep contours. Town gives way to country immediately, as it does also at Constitution Hill, the old way out to the north-east, so that in these two directions at least, Settle has rare characteristics. It is a very special place, much of it a Conservation Area, beneath its guardian hill of Castlebergh. If time and energy allow, a short but challenging climb by public paths to Castlebergh's summit provides rewarding and panoramic views, particularly of the limestone landscapes to the north and west. Not least of Settle's amenities is a large free carpark on the south side of the town, a few minutes' walk from the market place.

Sedbergh

This is the largest town within the National Park, and since 1974 it has belonged to Cumbria. Only 5 miles from the M6 (Junction 37), it is the main western entrance to the Dales, and its situation on the A684 Northallerton–Kendal road has brought additional traffic through the town and increased its potential as a tourist centre from which to explore not only the western dales but southern and eastern Lakeland too.

Above the north-eastern corner of the town Castlehaw was the site of a Norman motte-and-bailey castle so placed as to guard the east–west corridor of Garsdale and the north–south route along the Rawthey valley. This river flows down the eastern side of the Howgill Fells, and

Sedbergh is the only settlement along its short course before it joins the Lune 2 miles to the south-west. At the town centre is the parish church, with Norman origins, with a miniscule market place adjoining. The market charter dates from 1251, but the market each Wednesday, with a handful of stalls here and rather more in the Joss Lane car-park at the eastern end of Main Street, is a smaller affair than that at Settle. Along the Kendal road, on the town's western edge, the large livestock auction market is a lively place on most Wednesdays.

Like Settle, Sedbergh experienced a period of industrial growth at the end of the eighteenth century when the local domestic knitting-trade, long established, was supplemented by a cotton industry based on mills built at Birks, Howgill and Millthrop. Two miles north-east of the town the Quaker Robert Foster built Hebblethwaite Hall Woollen Mill in 1792, 'for the better employment of the poor, established a school for their education, and became a mixture of father, physician, lawyer and judge amongst his dependants'. Foster's eldest son, Miles, subsequently became the father of the artist Birket Foster. After Robert Foster's retirement in 1812 the estate was sold, including 'the Mansion House, a good Farmhouse, and outbuildings; also Mills, and other conveniences now used in, and well adapted for, carrying on the Woollen Manufacture'. Although it did not pass into his own hands, a Joseph Dover, of a Keswick family, subsequently managed Hebblethwaite Mill, which prospered, and in 1837 he built Farfield Mill by the River Clough, leaving Hebblethwaite to become a bobbin- and saw-mill, but later to become ruinous. Today, very little remains, but the early Georgian farmhouse of Hebblethwaite Hall survives.

Turnpike Acts of 1761 brought about improvements to the Askrigg–Kendal and Lancaster–Kirkby Stephen roads, both passing through Sedbergh, which grew at the expense of Dent, until then the more important township. During the last third of the eighteenth century Sedbergh took on the appearance it now has, with many cobbled yards leading secretively off Main Street. These were crammed with cottages and two-storey houses with living accommodation upstairs and ground floors let out as stores and stables. King's Yard off the north side, and Weavers' Yard and Railton Yard off the south side of Main Street exemplify, if in a run-down form, these developments, with No 5 Railton Yard retaining its wooden spinning-gallery.

Undoubtedly the most far-reaching event in Sedbergh's history was the founding by Roger Lupton, a native of the town and then Provost of Eton, of a chantry school which he endowed with scholarships and fellowships at St John's College, Cambridge. Becoming a free grammar school in 1552 it was rebuilt in 1716 and again in the 1860s, prior to becoming a public school in 1874. School buildings of late Victorian date and extensive playing-fields cover much of Sedbergh's southern edge, and the cultural, academic and sporting reputations of the school have brought national fame, as well as employment and prosperity to Sedbergh. The distinctive 1716 building on the corner of the Dent road, now a library and museum, is the sole survivor of the earlier grammar school.

Sedbergh's strong Quaker associations – George Fox was a frequent visitor, his most famous preaching occasion being the great outdoor meeting at Firbank in 1652 – are appropriately illustrated at Brigflatts, originally a small industrial hamlet to the south-west. There, the delightful Friends' Meeting-House of 1675, the oldest in northern England, retains most of its original furnishings in an atmosphere of cool, tranquil beauty hallowed by three centuries of quiet devotion.

Hawes

This relative newcomer among Dales market towns did not receive its charter until 1700, but within the past thirty years seems to have been making up for lost time and has become a lively, thriving and important centre for trade and tourism. To a large extent this must be due to its unusual situation near the head of Wensleydale. Not only is Wensleydale the middle one of the three major valleys but it is the only one having a main road, the A684, running along its complete length, a convenient link between the A1 30 miles to the east and the M6 some 20 miles to the west. Additionally, the B6259 through Mallerstang gives good access to Kirkby Stephen, Appleby and the A66 to the north, while the B6255 links Hawes with Ingleton and, subsequently, via the A687, Lancaster, to the south-west. All these are Category II roads in the National Park Committee's 'Advisory Hierarchy on Roads' agreed in 1981. The Northallerton and Hawes branch of the North Eastern Railway, operating since 1877, and linked to the Settle–Carlisle line at Hawes Junction, now Garsdale station, gave Wensleydale the distinction of being the only valley in the area with a through east–west line, a situation which ended with its closure in 1964.

It was probably the growth of pack-horse trade which justified Hawes receiving its market charter, and a boost to this trade followed the rerouting of the important Richmond–Lancaster turnpike through the town in 1795. Until then, this had taken the tortuous route from

Askrigg, via Bainbridge, along the Roman road over Wether Fell and Cam to Gearstones and Ingleton. Steep gradients and restricted use caused by severe weather in winter necessitated an easier route, which is now followed by the present A684 from Bainbridge and the B6255 up Widdale. Farming was always the main activity in Wensleydale, and there is no doubt that improved roads contributed to Hawes' growing importance as a marketing centre for livestock, and later for the locally produced butter and cheese. In addition, hand-knitting was a flourishing local industry with the hamlets of Gayle, Appersett, Burtersett, Hardraw and Sedbusk supplying large quantities of goods, particularly stockings. Until the eighteenth century West Riding merchants brought wool to these places for spinning, but from the 1780s small mills at Gayle, Hawes and Burtersett introduced machinery to the area. A cotton-mill was built at Gayle in 1784, and more small mills at Hawes, above and below the bridge, within the next few years. But upper Wensleydale was too remote to enable it to compete with other areas where canals and, later, railways provided much better communication and more readily available supplies of coal for steam power.

The area in Hawes around Gayle Beck was probably the nucleus of the original village, but date panels on a few houses in the market place indicate occupation there before the market charter. Rose House (1692) and Cockett's near-by (1668), both on the north side of the market place, are genuine seventeenth-century buildings, but at the house called Town Head, on the south side, beyond the school, the lintel dated 1643 is misleading, being a recent insertion. Near the market hall an enclosure called Penny Garth, now used as a carpark, was formerly part of the market area used as a street auction for livestock. Last century this included geese, sold in autumn by local folk to an Askrigg dealer, who tarred and sanded their feet to make them suitable for long-distance travel. Thus shod they were walked, five or six hundred at a time, down Wensleydale to Middleham, Masham, Thirsk and even York, gradually being sold to farmers who required the geese to graze their stubble fields after harvest. A small shop, now a butcher's, near Penny Garth, served as a booth for the collection of market tolls.

As with other market towns old corners survive, their local names illustrating former trades – Dyers' Garth, Gruel Street, Hatters' Yard, Penn Lane and Printers' Square. But much of the town dates from the coming of the railway, when there was a rapid, though limited, eastwards expansion. Some market-place shops have fronts also dating from the last quarter of the century, and many older houses were enlarged or refronted about the same time, including the former King

Edward Grammar School, founded in 1729, but now housing the post office.

Hawes Bridge is passed over more than looked at, but retains traces of its original pack-horse structure beneath the present arch. Upstream to the west is the former site of the Wensleydale Cheese Factory, used at the turn of the century after Edward Chapman had moved there from the smaller mill building, now the Conservative Club, just below the bridge. This was formerly the Hawes Corn Mill, whose east wall shows scars of its former water-wheel. Hawes church is a rather undistin-guished Victorian (1851) replacement of a smaller chapel opposite the White Hart, a handsome late Georgian coaching-inn and staging-post used by the Northallerton–Kendal coaches in the early decades of last century.

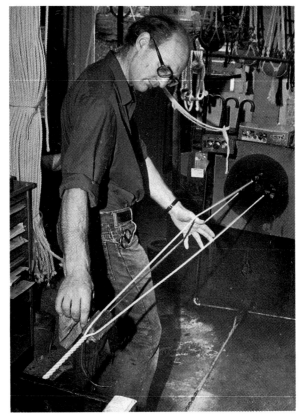

Hawes Ropeworks. Norman Chapman using a grooved wooden top to keep the three separate strands apart while the twist is put into a rope. The twisting machine (right) revolves, and as the strands twist they become shorter, pulling the sledge (left) forward

The premises of the former railway station now house a National Park information centre, open daily from Easter to October, with an interpretative display arranged in the former booking office. Near-by, the old engine shed has been thoughtfully adapted for use as the Upper Dales Folk Museum, which displays an ever-increasing range of exhibits covering all aspects of life and work in the area – farming, lead-mining, quarrying, local crafts and trades, as well as veterinary equipment. Based on material collected over the years by Askrigg authors and local historians Marie Hartley and Joan Ingilby this is a major exhibition of bygones of the upper dales, and is open in the afternoon from Easter to September. A small admission charge is made. Appropriately close, by the entrance to the station yard carpark, is the Hawes Ropeworks. Hawes has been noted for ropeworking certainly since 1841 and possibly considerably earlier. Based originally at the Old Toll Bar, now the Gate House, on the Ingleton road, it moved to its present premises at Town Foot in 1922, the Outhwaites having taken over the business in 1905 and continuing as ropemakers until 1975. Then, two college lecturers, Peter and Ruth Annison, bought the business and extended the range of products beyond those for farming use into the realms of household items, handicrafts, travel and leisure. New jobs have been created and the premises have gradually been enlarged. In 1981 Mr Outhwaite's original wooden shed was replaced by a newer one providing a longer rope-walk.

Leyburn

Although Leyburn is a little over 2 miles outside the National Park boundary, it has importance as a market and trading centre for much of Wensleydale and the area around, which is the reason for its inclusion here. In market terms alone it is almost a newcomer, like Hawes, its charter having been granted in 1684 to the Marquis of Winchester, later the Duke of Bolton. It is likely that Leyburn had steadily grown in importance after the decline of Wensley from about a century earlier. For a long period Leyburn was merely a hamlet in Wensley parish, with only a chapel of ease, and probably a few dwellings in or near the area now called Grove Square.

As its market grew, the Grove Square site was found to be too small, and the present spacious market place evolved around 1800, when the local corn market had become one of the most important in the North of England. Like Settle on the southern edge of the Park area, Leyburn was at a meeting point between two farming disciplines – stock-rearing to the west, and arable in the lower, drier lands to the east. Given good communications, market towns so placed almost always flourished. Leyburn's access from the north and south-east were not perfect, but the Richmond–Lancaster turnpike of 1751 soon threw off a branch through Bellerby to Leyburn, so that the town was linked to the north-east, the rich corn-lands of Durham, and the ports of the coast.

The market place was cobbled in about 1800, and parts of it still are. The stocks and market-cross vanished about twenty years later, by when many of the two- and three-storey buildings along the north and south sides had entered the scene, their commercial use indicating Leyburn's growing importance during Regency and early Victorian times. Very few original shop frontages have survived the late-twentieth-century onslaught, to the town's discredit, but many upper storeys retain windows of classical proportions, with glazing-bars, including an unusually high proportion of blocked-up windows with the outline of these bars painted white on black masonry. They may not necessarily represent a natural desire to avoid the window-tax (1695–c1850) but were more likely intended to keep the sense of visual balance of a façade, so important in pre-Victorian days.

The Bolton Arms typifies the period and enjoys a splendid situation at the upper, western end of the market place as well as a southern view across Wensleydale. Its neighbour, Leyburn Hall, shares this prospect, but it is unfortunate that this, the town's finest building, probably of the mid-eighteenth century, is completely hidden from any viewpoint in the town, although its elegant south front can be seen from the road out to the west. Dominating the market place is the large town hall, which, although as late as 1856, still shows Regency overtones. Its island site separates the main market-place area from a smaller square to the west, from where Shawl Terrace links the town with the open countryside so superbly seen from the Shawl.

This is a natural terrace on limestone turf running 2 miles westward, its unusual name possibly derives from 'shaw', meaning 'copse'. In early Victorian times it was laid out as a promenade with seats and shelters, but now only two or three seats remain. Few towns have so rewarding a viewpoint so easily reached, but it is worth while continuing the walk along the ash and hazel groves for the increasingly quiet and sylvan nature of the landscape.

Back in the town, Grove Square is smaller and more intimate than the market place. Alleyways leading from it reveal early industrial buildings and workshops, while at the top end of the square Thornborough Hall, a late Georgian house drastically altered to Jacobean style in 1863, now houses the District Council offices, courtroom and library. In woodland beyond, and above some restrained modern housing for old people, morning sunlight gleams on a tiny, sham-medieval castle, a little garden folly.

On the Bellerby road leading northwards from the town, the auction market of 1917 has gradually increased its throughput of stock and, like that at Hawes, is a limited company with mainly local farmers as shareholders. A large market place makes a town feel friendly, and on Fridays Leyburn market place is full of colourful stalls, which, especially during the holiday season, attract hundreds of visitors who find the town a good starting-point for a journey into the Dales or a good centre in which to stay while exploring them. Although it has no single out-standing building – none of its churches is earlier than 1835 – it has good groups, interesting roof-lines and a pleasant textural variety that gives it visual appeal.

Pateley Bridge

Although Nidderdale was excluded from the National Park it is still one of the major dales, a favourite with many visitors – perhaps precisely for one of the reasons for its omission, namely its two large reservoirs of Scar House and Gouthwaite, with their restricted access. Pateley Bridge is Nidderdale's own market town, occupying a favour-ably sheltered situation on the north bank of the Nidd, on the frontier between upland and lowland farming.

In medieval times monastic estates in and around the valley helped to promote good communications so that it was almost inevitable that a market centre would evolve, particularly at this important river cros-sing on a trading route leading from the Craven uplands, via Gras-sington, to Fountains Abbey and Ripon. So Pateley steadily prospered from the fourteenth century, reaching a peak in about 1800, but when the textile industry turned to steam-power the old water-powered mills of Nidderdale could not compete. Local linen manufacture declined and the mills were adapted to make cord, twine and rope. However, lead-mining on Greenhow Hill to the west not only survived but flourished last century, and quarrying of local gritstone for building ex-panded with the arrival of the railway in the 1860s. The Nidderdale line played an important part in the life of the dale for a century, and the Nidd Valley Light Railway of 1904, which had a thirty-year life, was constructed by Bradford Corporation for the building of the reservoirs. It linked Pateley with the dale head and carried thousands of visitors as well as construction material.

Pateley's present prosperity is based mainly on tourism and agriculture, and its fortnightly livestock market survives. Buildings of dark gritstone give a dour appearance to the town, which is aligned along a single main street leading northwards from the river. High above the town is its only medieval structure, the old church of St Mary, now sadly ruinous, having been abandoned in 1827 when its successor was built in a more convenient situation. Nearby, the Panorama Walk commands magnificent views of Nidderdale and its embracing moors, and in the town the recently established Nidderdale Museum displays a good collection of folk exhibits. Across the river the early-sixteenth-century Bewerley Chapel formerly belonged to Fountains Abbey, while on the moors to the north-east Brimham Rocks, which now belong to the National Trust, are one of the most dramatic areas of gritstone outcrops in Britain, and have been a tourist attraction for over two centuries.

7
NATURAL HISTORY

Long before life clothed and animated the Dales landscape, the underlying rocks were present and they still remain as the oldest form of
natural history. We have seen how they impart a distinctive character
to different parts of the area, recognised in scenic changes which occur
as you travel from one part of the area to another, even from one valley
to the next, especially if this means crossing a watershed. Where there
is gritstone there are sombre moors, dark for much of the year but burst-
ing into purple splendour usually during the second half of August with
the flowering of the heather. Limestone country, however, has a light-
ness, a greenness, a delicacy of tone and colour and detail that is in
marked contrast to moorland landscapes. You do not need to have the
expertise of a botanist or biologist to appreciate such scenic differences
and colour contrasts, but if you recognise them and perhaps wonder
why they occur you are beginning to touch the science of ecology and
the awareness of habitat. The study of the relationship of living things
to their environment and to one another is a relatively new scientific
discipline. Certainly John Constable would not have heard of it, or of
conservation, yet his oft-quoted words 'To know is to see', although he
was thinking in terms of art, apply equally to an appreciation of natural
history.

The accompanying map identifies a number of landscape zones, each
having a natural and/or man-made beauty, each providing its range of
wildlife habitats and contributing to the rich diversity of character of
the area. It is this natural beauty, the wealth of flora and fauna, of

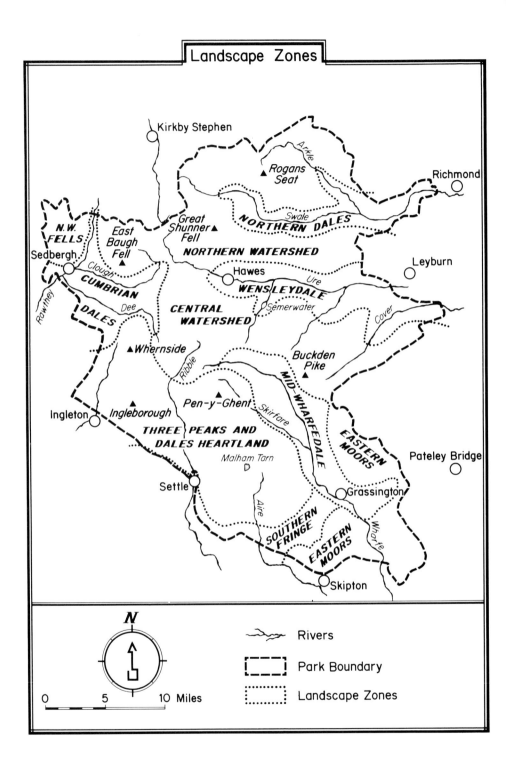

Landscape Zones

Kirkby Stephen

Richmond

Arkle

Rogans
Seat ▲

Swale

NORTHERN DALES

N.W.
FELLS

East
Baugh
Fell ▲

Great
Shunner ▲
Fell

NORTHERN WATERSHED

Leyburn

Sedbergh

Clough

CUMBRIAN

Hawes

WENSLEYDALE

Ure

Rawthey

Dee

DALES

**CENTRAL
WATERSHED**

Semerwater

Cover

▲Whernside

Ribble

Buckden
Pike ▲

MID-WHARFEDALE

Ingleborough ▲

Pen-y-Ghent ▲

Skirfare

**EASTERN
MOORS**

Ingleton

**THREE PEAKS AND
DALES HEARTLAND**

Malham Tarn

Pateley Bridge

Settle

Aire

**SOUTHERN
FRINGE**

Grassington

**EASTERN
MOORS**

Wharfe

Skipton

N

0   5   10 Miles

Rivers

Park Boundary

Landscape Zones

geological and physiographic features, which the National Park Committee has a statutory duty to preserve and enhance. It is worth considering in turn each of these landscape zones with reference to their non-human life.

The Northern and Central Watersheds

Moorlands of Millstone Grit sweep down the centre of the Park from north to south, forming a spine from which radiate the surrounding dales. In the north these moors curve round to form a natural northern boundary of the Park, and in the centre their east–west alignment creates a formidable boundary between Wensleydale and Wharfedale. Huge areas of gritstone moors, mainly above 1,400ft (427m), dark in appearance, dreary to tramp across and dour even to drivers, present an environment hostile to man, a wilderness landscape of sombre beauty. You can experience its character in a journey from one valley to another, either on foot or by car. Any of the routes out of upper Swaledale illustrate it, as does the journey by Yorkshire's highest road, between Hawes and upper Wharfedale, which crosses the central watershed at Fleet Moss, 1,932ft (589m).

This name is significant, for mosses (bogs), many of them named on the map, characterise these lonely uplands. Vegetation is remarkably uniform, and plant species are few, with cotton-grass dominating. In early summer this attractive plant merits the name, its white, cottony, fruiting heads lightening the landscape of peat-hags, dark bogs and heather moor. The basal sheaths of cotton-grass, being rich in potash and nitrogen, provide sheep with an early 'bite' in spring. Other common plants of these upland mosses are related to the wet conditions; while cross-leaved heather, bilberry and crowberry prosper on better-drained land, together with some sedges, rushes and grasses.

Peat itself is formed largely from the remains of cotton-grass, and has accumulated steadily since about 5000BC. Various tree seeds incorporated in it indicate the existence of early woodlands at much higher levels than at present. It is the spongy nature of peat which regulates the flow of water through a moss, one result of which is that becks draining from it tend to dry up only in extreme drought conditions. When peat does dry out, the cotton-grass gradually dies and the moss degenerates to become a dry moor favouring heather and bilberry. Lead-mining activities of the seventeenth and eighteenth centuries sometimes accelerated the draining of mosses, as did the work of gamekeepers in charge of grouse moors last century.

Today, in these upland areas of high rainfall, current systems of land management involve improving the drainage of many mosses. Moorland gripping, as it is called, means the cutting of open ditches, usually in the parallel lines of herring-bone pattern, to supplement existing drainage channels. The visual effect of gripping is apparent in the view from many upland roads, particularly on the descent from Fleet Moss into Langstrothdale, above Garsdale and Dentdale, and around Cam Houses. The Nature Conservancy Council is disturbed by the damage caused to some upland habitats as a result of gripping, particularly in very boggy areas and where there is deep peat. Additionally, the quicker run-off of surface water which arises can cause damage to cave systems in the limestone beneath, with consequent danger for pothollers. Moorland gripping is sometimes blamed for the flash floods which occasionally occur at lower levels.

Heather moors occupy the zone which extends downwards from the cotton-grass mosses to the rough grazing, and although they commonly occur at 1,000–1,400ft (305–427m), they reach as high as 1,700ft (518m) in the northern watersheds, dropping to about 700ft (213m) where the ridges descend as long spurs to the eastern margins. Indeed, the acid rocks of these uplands, mainly 900–1,400ft (274–427m) high, support thousands of acres of moorland dominated by heather and bracken. It is no coincidence that, above Bolton Abbey in lower Wharfedale, and above Reeth in Swaledale, public access is widespread, largely because these areas are so visually spectacular during the peak holiday month of August.

Most of this moorland is, however, common grazing. In early spring, when other food is scarce, sheep find rich nourishment in young heather, and to ensure a good supply of fresh growth sensible moormanagement is necessary. Old heather needs to be controlled by careful burning – too much, or over-liming, or over-draining affects the ecological balance and mat-grass, which has little or no nutritious value, takes over. Where bracken tends to invade the heather, grazing by cattle helps to keep this in check. Grouse like not only heather shoots but also the older heather which provides good shelter. Thus, gamekeeper and shepherd to some extent have similar aims in moor-management.

Grasses grow along the sheep-cropped moor edges, with white mat-grass dominant. Where damper soils encourage it, blue moor-grass flourishes, while among the other grasses are sheep's fescue, silver hair-grass and common bent. Tormentil, milkwort, spearwort, knapweed and eyebrights add splashes of colour, but it is the leguminous trefoils and vetches which provide the greater pasturage value of grassy moorland sward by many roadsides – tempting areas for visitors to park their cars and enjoy the quiet beauty.

Most commercial afforestation in the Dales occurs on the slopes of upper valleys in the central and northern watersheds. Compared with much of upland Britain the Yorkshire Dales has relatively little land under coniferous plantations – around 7,500 acres (3,000ha). However, 80 per cent of this (6,000 acres/2,400ha) has been planted since 1966, much of it in the remote valley of Langstrothdale in the central watershed, not traversed by a through motor road, although very prominent from the Cam Road and Pennine Way. Motorists are more likely to notice the smaller though still extensive plantations in Widdale above Hawes, in Dentdale and Garsdale, and – if they venture into their quiet delights – Cotterdale and Walden. Three constraints limit the amount of afforestation: (1) much of the land is above 1,000ft (305m) with high ground often very exposed; (2) over most of the limestone areas of the Three Peaks and Dales heartland zone, soils are shallow and alkaline; (3) 28 per cent of the land within the Park is common land, with little prospect of forestry expansion.

The National Park Committee has recently prepared an afforestation policy with guidelines intended to be applied to all new proposals. The main aim of the policy is to conserve the essential character of the various areas of the Park. To some extent this may seem a case of wisdom after the event, for in some locations the damage has been done. Langstrothdale will never be the same again, and the wild beauty of Cotterdale has largely disappeared beneath a dark coniferous blanket. But lessons have been learned, so it is hoped that future commercial afforestation will be rigorously controlled. Where it is allowed, far more careful consideration needs to be given to the location and shape of plantations.

Bird life of the central and northern watersheds is characteristic of most upland fell country. Moorland birds are more distinctive than those of the valleys, limestone pastures and woodlands, but there are fewer species. A typical stretch of moorland can support twenty to fifty birds in every 100 acres (40ha), a figure which should be seasonally adjusted, for winter numbers would be fewer.

No sound is more evocative of the wild, damp uplands than the curlew's bubbling call, particularly in early spring and summer. Golden plover, redshank and snipe join them, while sandpipers and oystercatchers are becoming more common along the upper reaches of becks and around the high tarns which now have large breeding-colonies of black-headed gulls. Summer Lodge Tarn, Whitaside Tarn and Locker

Tarn, all on the fells between Swaledale and Wensleydale, support hundreds of breeding pairs, while Birkdale Tarn near Keld and the various tarns on Whernside all have their resident populations. Among the birds of prey, most are just about holding their own, although you need to know where to expect peregrines, merlins and short-eared owls. Buzzards, however, are more common.

Unusually, it is one of the smallest birds, the meadow-pipit, which probably has the widest habitat range, extending from the high fells to rough grazings at low levels, with a fairly consistent distribution of up to ten birds per 100 acres (40ha). Provided there is some ground cover skylarks can be expected at all but the highest altitudes, while swifts and swallows swoop over the summer uplands far from their nesting-sites in and around buildings. Once their breeding season is over, starlings tend to flock upwards to the moors. It is, of course, the red grouse which is the most characteristic and certainly the noisiest of the birds of the heather moor, its rasping call a repeated give-away of its presence, its rapid, whirring flight and heather-tuft perch a source of constant delight.

The Three Peaks and Dales Heartland

In the landscape zone described as the 'Three Peaks and Dales Heartland' the Great Scar Limestone dominates the scene. Its weathering has created features unique in Britain both in form and extent: limestone pavements, cliffs and scars on the surface matched by remarkable cave systems, potholes and streams below ground. Wide, sweeping, spacious landscapes of limestone country blend into rich pastures and valley meadows, against which the Millstone Grit caps of the Three Peaks stand out as familiar and dramatic landmarks. Woodlands are few and small but visually important; villages intrude minimally; field barns and stone walls have greater impact. Limestone soils may be shallow but man's historic imprint is deep; today, the limestone heartlands attract the greatest number of visitors.

Ecologically, limestone country differs from gritstone moorland in two distinct ways. Its plant life is richer and far more diversified, not dominated by either of the species, heather and cotton-grass, which characterise the moors, giving them broad areas of tone and colour. As a result, limestone landscapes are more delicately toned, harmonious in greys, silvers and greens. Pearly-grey outcrops of rock, tree-fringed along straight-etched scars, alternate with broad masses of good green grassland of pasture and meadow. The rock surfaces of scars and pavements, as well as the rich turf, support a wide range of flowers and trees. Unusually, flowers of the limestone seem to be more brightly coloured than elsewhere.

Limestone plants fall into three groups: those of the grasslands and limestone pavements; plants of the limestone scars and associated woods; woodland plants of lower limestone slopes. The Great Scar Limestone of the Dales heartland predominates over the Craven uplands, from Wharfedale to Ribblesdale, extending westwards to the lesser-known but beautiful valleys of Crummackdale and Kingsdale. Additionally, limestones occur in Wensleydale and Swaledale in association with the sandstones and shales of the Yoredale Series, so that these valleys have their limestone flora, together with plants of more acid soils, contributing to the very rich variety of plants in these northern dales.

Limestone grasslands formerly supported a cover of scrub and open broad-leaved woodland which is now limited to the scars. Exposure and thin soils inhibit tree growth, as Walter Morrison discovered on his Malham Tarn House estates around the middle of last century. Of the million trees he planted on Malham Moor only 5 per cent have survived, mostly in a rather stunted form. Spread of grassland over the Craven limestone uplands was encouraged in medieval times by monastic landowners whose grazing flocks reduced any colonisation by trees. Continued grazing since then has ensured the grassland's survival; grassland sets the scene and grasses are the main plants.

Sheep's fescue is usually dominant. With sweet vernal grass, hairy oat and crested dog's tail it has a high nutritional value, far more so than other grasses of the limestone – false oat, quaking grass and the two brome grasses. The dry nature of well-drained grasslands brings the added advantage of discouraging foot-rot and liver-fluke, two of the main diseases affecting sheep. For almost eight centuries the Craven sheep walks have supported huge flocks; numbers may have dwindled, but sheep-voices continue to call across the cloud-dappled pastures from Ribblesdale to Wharfedale.

Limestone pavements of the Craven heartlands account for almost half of the total area of such features in Britain. These remarkable, visually distinctive areas of bare limestone blocks, or 'clints', separated by fissures called 'grykes', are of such geological and ecological importance that many are designated Sites of Special Scientific Interest (SSSIs). Two are National Nature Reserves – Colt Park Wood and Scar Close, both on the northern flanks of Ingleborough, near Ribble Head – while another, Souther Scales Pavement, is managed as a nature reserve by

Limestone pavement at Souther
Scales, Chapel-le-Dale, on the
western flanks of Ingleborough

the Yorkshire Wildlife Trust. Best known is undoubtedly the extraordi-
nary pavement above Malham Cove, poised above the great inland
cliff, and crossed dramatically by the Pennine Way. Less known but
very much more extensive are the vast areas of pavement extending
above Crummackdale eastwards across the strange hill called
Moughton.

Usually no soil survives on limestone pavements. Only lichens and
mosses cling to the bare stone, but in the damp, shady fissures soil
accumulates, encouraging some plants and ferns to thrive, untroubled
by summer's heat or animals grazing, each gryke an ecosystem re-
sembling a miniature gorge. An assemblage of woodland plants can be
expected, with dog's mercury, wood-anemone, wood-sorrel, ramsons,
herb-Robert, green spleenwort, holly-fern and hart's tongue fern.
Occasionally trees survive, more often as individual hawthorns or
elder, but Colt Park Wood is one of the best British examples of an
aboriginal limestone scar ashwood. Although ash is dominant many
other species thrive, including willow, hazel, birch, bird-cherry,
mountain ash, guelder-rose, hawthorn and elder. Additionally, there is
remarkable ground flora of over 150 species identified in the 21 acres
(8.5ha) of the wood. The trees grow on the clints, their roots penetrat-

ing into the grykes, and in spite of so precarious a foothold the ash trees at the wood's northern end have grown to almost 40ft (12m), although the wood thins out, with plant cover decreasing towards the south. A permit from the Nature Conservancy is required to visit this reserve.

At Scar Close near-by the pavement must at one time have been covered with peat, most of which has now vanished, so that there are only a few small pockets left. These support lime-hating plants like heather, closely associated with lime-lovers such as lily-of-the-valley. A similar anomaly occurs on Fawcett Moor, south-east of Penyghent, where cotton-grass, heather and bilberry grow close to limestone outcrops with their calcareous flora. On Moughton, above Austwick, juniper grows in some quantity, although, judging by the increasing number of dead bushes, bleached to the colour of the rock beneath, little natural regeneration seems to be taking place.

Limestone scars and cliffs are characteristic features of the Dales heartland as well as of Wensleydale and mid-Wharfedale, and these show a rich variety of plant life. At lower levels trees and shrubs fringe these scars, well appreciated in the view from the road up Wharfedale between Grassington and Buckden, and along both sides of Wensleydale being especially prominent between Aysgarth and Bainbridge, with a 2 mile stretch of scar wood near Thornton Rust having only one small break in it, at Cubeck, where a minor road cuts through the low limestone cliff. The south side of Littondale has a fine scar wood extending for 1½ miles between Arncliffe and Litton. Smaller scar woods occur in Swaledale, around Gunnerside and Keld, in the Chapel-le-Dale area, on the southern flanks of Ingleborough near Austwick and Feizor, while motorists travelling on the A65 west of Settle cannot fail to see the splendid wood which clothes much of Giggleswick Scar to the north of the road.. All these examples occur at heights of between 700ft and 1,000ft (210m and 305m).

Although ash is invariably present in scar woods, hazel is usually dominant. Associated trees and shrubs include mountain ash, hawthorn, blackthorn, bird-cherry and holly, with raspberry, elder, guelder-rose and other wild roses. Sycamores are less common. Shade in scar woods allows a normal woodland flora, while sufficient depth of soil accumulates on the many grass-covered ledges to encourage limestone plants to flourish. Thus, scar woods provide a range of habitats supporting a diverse flora. Grass Wood in mid-Wharfedale is a scar wood extending up to limestone pavement. Partly a nature reserve managed by the Yorkshire Wildlife Trust, it has a public right-of-way through it. Ash is dominant, but plantations of beech, sycamore and conifer have been added. A particularly rich flora has almost four hundred plant species recorded in Grass Wood with its neighbour, Bastow Wood, and exploring the rather rough terrain in the fullness of spring is a rewarding experience.

On higher scars, for example the rocky ledges and cliffs near the summits of Ingleborough and Penyghent where the limestone is immediately below the Millstone Grit, other plant assemblages occur. Dwarf willow, hoary whitlow grass, vernal sandwort, yellow mountain saxifrage, purple saxifrage, and occasionally some maritime species like thrift and sea-campion have all been recorded on these high scars, seen only by walkers and climbers who delight in their windy solitude and wide views.

The area around Ribble Head and Ingleborough's northern slopes claims to be the only British habitat of the Yorkshire sandwort, first identified in 1889 at Ribble Head station. Near-by, in the damp limestone pastures around the upper waters of the Ribble, by Gayle Beck and in Thorns Gill, globeflower and bird's-eye primrose thrive, but not in such profusion as I have seen in Bardale, above Semerwater. A tiny wood, only ½ acre, (0.2ha), by the roadside a mile west of Malham Tarn, has been a Yorkshire Wildlife Trust nature reserve since 1963. Globeflower Wood is a fine example of marsh-moor habitat, and although it takes its name from a particular plant, its seasonal flora is extremely rich, easily appreciated by merely looking over the roadside wall. No additional access is necessary; nor is it allowed, so that neither humans nor livestock can disturb the natural balance and beauty, probably at its best around the middle of June. Meadow-sweet, melancholy thistle, water avens, wood-cranesbill and giant bellflower are other plants favouring damp limestones pastures, while by contrast, vernal sandwort, white, delicate and tiny, seems to be the first flower successfully to colonise the arid spoil-heaps of lead-mining areas.

Limestone landscapes of the Dales heartland have an open, spacious quality, a peacefulness and visual splendour which many visitors find particularly appealing and inspiring. Visitor pressure on these limestone areas is tremendous, and erosion is becoming more and more evident. But wear and tear by human feet is not the only threat to limestone uplands. Unsympathetic modern farming methods can seriously affect diversity of habitats; quarrying gouges huge chunks of limestone fell – at Horton, Giggleswick, Kilnsey and Threshfield – while manmade features such as field barns and boundary walls, if neglected, decline into disrepair and dereliction.

The National Park Authority employs a wide range of techniques to try to protect and conserve the natural and historical landscapes. These include planning controls, conservation advice for farmers and landowners, and the presentation of formal and informal educational programmes for the public, particularly through audio-visual and interpretative displays at National Park Centres. Additionally, over the past few years the National Park Authority has made generous grants towards the acquisition of land for nature reserves. Physical conservation work such as tree planting, footpath maintenance and habitat management forms an important part of each year's conservation programme, not only in the Dales heartland where some of the pressures are greatest, but throughout the whole Park.

The Northern Dales, Wensleydale and mid-Wharfedale

Broad-leaved trees, either as shelter-belts or in small woodlands, impart a more sylvan nature to these landscape zones, which are dominated by the Carboniferous Limestone and have valley floors of flat meadowland with permanent pasture up the lower slopes of the hills. In addition to the scar woods described, many tributary valleys are characterised by hanging woods or gill woods. Most of the deciduous woodlands are man-made additions to the landscape, originating in some cases in the Middle Ages, when monastic and lay landowners planted oaks, usually as part of their deer-parks. Some trees in the Valley of Desolation, near Bolton Abbey, may be survivors of those days. From the middle of the eighteenth century landowners planted trees for visual appeal, to provide cover for game or as shelter-belts. These have matured to constitute a high proportion of today's tree cover, but over the years this has gradually diminished. Most of the important woods or groups of woods are less than 10 acres (4ha) in size, although about 150 woodlands are larger than this, with a few over 100 acres (40ha).

The National Park Committee recognises the importance of traditional broad-leaved woodland, gives high priority to its conservation and offers positive assistance to the management of such woods, both financial and practical. Currently, two main schemes are operated:

(1) Ninety per cent grant aid is available to landowners who wish to plant small areas, involving costs to the National Park Committee of less than £500 each. Between 1977 and 1985, 268 projects were approved, with grant aid totalling £44,500.
(2) For larger projects seventy five per cent grant aid is payable and in the same period seventy four schemes have cost the committee £50,700.

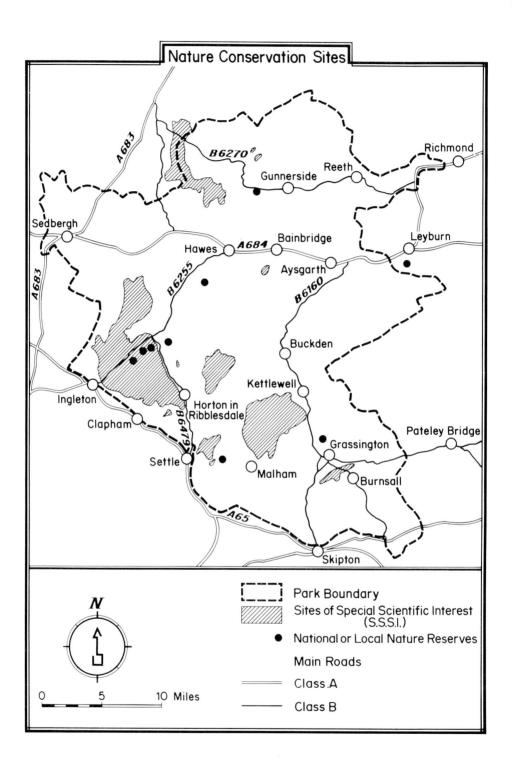

Nature Conservation Sites

Richmond

A683

B6270

Gunnerside   Reeth

Sedbergh

Hawes   A684   Bainbridge

B6255   Aysgarth   Leyburn

B6160

Buckden

Kettlewell

Ingleton

Horton in
Ribblesdale

Clapham   B6479

Settle   Malham

Grassington   Pateley Bridge

Burnsall

A65

Skipton

A683

N

0   5   10 Miles

Park Boundary

Sites of Special Scientific Interest
(S.S.S.I.)

● National or Local Nature Reserves

Main Roads

Class A

Class B

Most plantings under these schemes have involved small areas – usually less than 2.5 acres (1ha), although some have been specially designed to hide intrusive buildings, quarries and caravan sites. One plantation – at Thwaite Bridge, by the A684 west of Hawes – has a 5 acre (2ha) landslip area planted with three thousand trees to stabilise the slope as well as to enhance a bare corner of landscape. British Trust for Conservation Volunteers helped with this work. Hedgerow trees, small spinneys and copses, often at risk, can be encouraged. Valley landscapes throughout the Dales can scarcely be imagined without their trees, but natural regeneration cannot be relied upon to maintain the harmony. Even in some gill woods, where grazing by stock is minimal, broadleaved tree cover is declining.

These woodlands, occurring where becks cut ravines – not always apparent from the main roads – down valley sides, are an echo of ancient tree cover. In their still, shady atmosphere, trees grow tall, seeking the sunlight, and there are always sounds of water. In Swaledale gill woods commonly occur near Healaugh, above Gunnerside, and around Keld, with more good examples at Oxnop and by the road to Summer Lodge. Wensleydale has splendid gill woods, with Whitfield Gill near Askrigg outstanding. A public footpath west of the parish church leads to Mill Gill and Whitfield Gill, where the impressive ravine has fine waterfalls as well as mature beeches. Ash is dominant, however, but at higher levels shares a more open habitat with birch, holly, hawthorn and some oak and larch, while at the top of the gill a small ash wood reaches up steep contours to the foot of Whitfield Scar, with the highest trees at about 1,500ft (450m), possibly the highest broad-leaved wood in the Dales.

Gill woods in Wensleydale and Swaledale, occurring on the Yoredale Series of rocks, include trees growing on shale and the instability of such slopes causes many fine trees to fall. Whitfield Gill, near my home and therefore the gill wood most familiar to me, has suffered greatly in this respect, with very little obvious natural regeneration, particularly of ash. It is probable that a similar situation exists with the other gill woods, but most of these are on private land, not traversed by public rights-of-way, and in the distant view may appear to be flourishing. The true picture may not be so rosy.

Bishopdale, Wensleydale's main tributary valley, carries the B6160 from West Burton to Buckden in Wharfedale and, in its upper reaches, shows many narrow gill woods. In the lower parts of the valley hedgerow trees soften the austerity, exemplified in the view from the minor road between Aysgarth and Thoralby; even more impressive is the panorama gained from Morphet Gate, on the old road above West Burton. Although this viewpoint involves a steep climb, the reward is immeasurable, embracing a superb wide view of Bishopdale and Wensleydale, and emphasising the importance of scattered broad-leaved trees in this beautiful Dales landscape.

In upper Ribblesdale, 2 miles east of Ribble Head, Ling Gill's importance as a gill wood has been recognised by the Nature Conservancy Council's designation of it as a National Nature Reserve. The Pennine Way crosses its northern extremity at Ling Gill bridge, and good viewpoints near-by allow walkers to appreciate its trees if not its ground flora. The reserve covers about 12 acres (5ha) of a wooded limestone ravine, about 1,000ft (305m) above sea-level, its steep sides obviously having protected it from grazing. Ash and hazel are dominant, with hawthorn, willow, mountain ash and aspen quite common. In the prevailing conditions of moisture and shade, fallen leaves provide a haven for woodland plants, including mountain-everlasting, globeflower, giant bellflower, herb-Paris, wood-cranesbill, melancholy thistle, marsh hawksbeard and wood forget-me-not, as well as many luxuriant ferns.

Globeflowers in Bardale

The Eastern Moors

By contrast with the gill woods, broad-leaved woodland of the eastern moors is characteristic of the Millstone Grit which outcrops at the south-eastern edge of the Park and extends beyond its boundaries into Nidderdale. Neither landscape zones nor landscapes themselves recognise administrative boundaries and some of the best oak woodlands occur on the eastern dip-slopes of the moors between lower Wensleydale and Nidderdale, typically represented by Carlesmoor and Dallowgill west of Kirkby Malzeard. Birk Gill, which joins Colsterdale 2½ miles west of Healey, makes an interesting comparison with Wensleydale's gill woods. In 1870 larch was dominant, with plenty of willows, hawthorns and oak in a heather-sided valley with outcropping boulders. With the exception of the larch the landscape here must have resembled that of earlier times before the present settlement pattern was established.

In the gritstone areas of the eastern moors, oak is dominant – the sessile variety which is characteristic of Pennine country. Lowland oak-woods commonly occur where soils are moist, deep and reasonably rich in humus, with resultant slight acidity. From lower Wensleydale, below Leyburn and thus outside the Park area, and continuing in a broad swathe southwards in the valleys draining the eastern moors – Colsterdale and lower Nidderdale in particular – oakwoods, with bluebells in spring, create their distinctive pattern. In Wharfedale they flourish throughout the lower dale, generally below Burnsall, and are usually restricted to land below the 500ft (152m) contour. Alder, ash, wych elm, sycamore and willow, together with the deliberately planted beech and larch, introduce a diversity of canopy and colour, especially in spring and autumn. Beneath the usual shrub layer of bramble, elder, hawthorn, hazel, holly and guelder-rose, there is usually rich ground flora, dominated by lesser celandine, wood-anemone, wood-sorrel, bluebell and ramsons. A walk through the Strid Woods Nature Trail near Bolton Abbey in spring illustrates this wild-flower splendour. A month later, near the carpark, a woodside meadow glories in a carpet of cowslips.

One habitat common to all the major dales is the valley grasslands, comprising hay-meadows and permanent pastures both on the fertile valley floors and extending up the hillsides, sometimes to above the 1,000ft (305m) contour. When they were managed traditionally these fields developed very rich floras, but with the marked increase in the use of inorganic fertilisers and herbicides, this floral richness has declined since the mid-1950s. In the past the quality of Dales grassland was maintained by natural manure from grazing stock, supplemented by the occasional use (every three years or so) of lime and basic slag on land that was reasonably accessible. Grant aid has, however, encouraged the use of chemical fertilisers, which are selective in their effect, favouring the growth of vigorous perennial grasses at the expense of less competitive species and many flowering plants. Additionally, Dales farmers are changing over from hay to silage, a process in which the grass is cut sooner – before flowering and setting seed – and which is also less dependent on good weather, as well as providing bulkier winter feed. In the uncertain climate of the Dales this makes good sense; in the uncertain economic conditions it may also make sense, albeit at a high visual cost.

A recent survey of hay-meadows showed that fewer than 5 per cent of the 3,750 meadows in the Park area were now farmed traditionally and retained their habitat value in terms of wild plants and animals. My own observations suggest that those in upper Swaledale, between Gunnerside and Keld, and especially around Muker, are the finest in the Dales. They are ideally revealed in late June or early July in an average year, from the field path between Muker and Thwaite, or in that most colourful of walks between Muker and the River Swale at Rampsholm. Recognition of the quality of Swaledale hay-meadows recently resulted in the acquisition by the Yorkshire Wildlife Trust of a small roadside field, Yelland's Meadow, as a nature reserve, to be managed under lease to a local farmer, who will continue to farm it by traditional methods. It is the first Dales meadow to be so designated, and the National Park Committee, the Countryside Commission and the World Wildlife Fund all made substantial contributions to its purchase.

At the same time, and helped in a similar way, the Yorkshire Wildlife Trust also acquired as a nature reserve a species-rich, south-facing sloping permanent pasture east of Wensley, just outside the Park area. The Old Glebe Field, covering about 10 acres (4ha) commands fine views across Wensleydale to Penhill, and its calcareous grassland contains over eighty species of plants. Among the most notable are green-winged and burnt-tip orchids, here close to their northern limit of distribution. Cowslips thrive in late spring, followed by a fine display of summer flowers. A simple management plan seeks to maintain the character of this important field, and a nature trail is planned.

These fields are only small, but the fact of their designation as nature reserves indicates an increasing awareness of the importance of conserving such habitats in the Park area. Probably the best known and

Yelland's Meadow, Muker, Swaledale in June 1984. This is a three-acre hay meadow farmed in the traditional way and now a nature reserve of the Yorkshire Wildlife Trust Ltd

most visited of all conservation habitats in the Yorkshire Dales is the Malham Tarn Estate, owned by the National Trust since 1946. For most of that period the Trust has leased it to the Field Studies Council, a national body with the aims of encouraging research and fieldwork in all branches of natural history, but particularly in the geology, flora and fauna of the Great Scar Limestone which gives the area its unique character.

The estate originally belonged to the Listers of Gisburn, who became the Lords Ribblesdale and in the late eighteenth century built Tarn House. Walter Morrison acquired this in 1856 and greatly extended it in a style reflecting the influence of his friend Ruskin. Malham Tarn House now accommodates several hundred students from schools and colleges every year and during the summer holidays courses suitable for family groups are run. Field studies are supplemented by laboratory work and among the subjects covered are the plant life of the limestone area, bird life on Malham Moor, geological studies and the freshwater life on Malham Tarn and the neighbouring becks.

The Southern Fringe

Limestone cliffs and scars mark the southern edge of the Great Scar Limestone along the line of the Craven Fault. Between it and the A65 there is a landscape zone – a narrow band between Settle and Threshfield – showing different characteristics. This lower-lying country, gently undulating in nature, is still mostly grassland, and contains some of the rare traditional parkland landscapes within the National Park area, linking it with the more industrialised areas beyond. At these lower altitudes, hedges have replaced the walls of the limestone country, hedgerow trees and small woodlands are more apparent, while winding lanes and field paths are the rule rather than the exception. The Pennine Way itself here takes a route across pastures, past small copses and over little drumlins as it approaches Gargrave. Map reading is perhaps more exacting than are the physical challenges which prevail farther north. As the Way follows the youthful River Aire to its source near Malham, the landscapes through which it passes are gentle, green hors d'oeuvres for the limestone delights to follow, and between Airton and Kirkby Malham the route passes one or two former mills and their associated houses, now likely to be country cottages for commuters or holidaying visitors.

The Cumbrian Dales

It will by now be apparent that the Yorkshire Dales National Park is not one landscape but many. It is possible, therefore, to visit just one of the nine zones and conclude, wrongly of course, that that particular area typifies the whole. An east–west journey, preferably by the A684 to the head of Wensleydale, crossing the watershed near the Moorcock Inn at Garsdale Head and continuing westwards into the narrow, confined trough of Garsdale itself, illustrates the dramatic change of landscape and buildings. Garsdale and its southern neighbour, Dentdale, look westwards towards distant Lakeland. Although they are both limestone valleys, with surrounding high ridges capped by Millstone Grit, their settlement patterns, their farming, their villages and farms, tend to resemble those in the Lake District. Dentdale is generously wooded, with small coniferous plantations darkening its hillsides, while Garsdale's upper reaches, as the views from the road testify, are quite heavily afforested with new plantations, although these diminish in number and size lower down the valley. Names of farms along the way – Knudmaning, Dandra Garth, Thursgill and Raygill – reflect the Norse settlement of a thousand years ago.

At Garsdale Foot the valley opens out, and the motorist driving westwards is rewarded by sweeping views of the Howgill Fells, smooth-flanked and sinuous above Sedbergh. Near the carpark on the north side of the road a lane – formerly part of the 1761 Sedbergh–Askrigg turnpike – leads down to Danny Bridge where the River Clough flows through an impressive limestone gorge and presently crosses the line of the Dent Fault. To mark the two-hundredth anniversary of the birth, in Dent in 1785, of the great geologist Adam Sedgwick, the National Park Authority has created a half-mile geology trail along the south side of the river, running westwards from Danny Bridge.

Another commemorative trail, inaugurated in 1970, recalls the great Victorian botanist and gardener Reginald Farrer (1880–1920). This nature trail is at Clapham, where Farrer was born and grew up in the family home, Ingleborough Hall. As a young man, he travelled extensively, in company with other enthusiastic botanists and collectors, in the Alps, Dolomites and the Far East, bringing back to Clapham fine specimens of plants, many of which he incorporated into his rock gardens based on local limestone. As a result of his travels, writings and collections, he became known as the 'Father of English rock gardening', and the Farrer Nature Trail passes through the grounds of the Hall, by the artificial lake created from the waters of Clapham Beck, and through woodland which includes Spanish chestnut, Corsican pine, holm-oak and bamboo – all introduced species.

At the south-eastern corner of the National Park, woodland is a

Garsdale, looking eastwards up the dale. This stretch of the River Clough below Danny Bridge is now part of the Sedgwick Geology Trail

prominent feature in the Strid Wood Nature Trail, near Bolton Abbey, where the trustees of the Chatsworth Settlement have created self-guided walks. They were not the first to do so there, for in the early decades of last century the Rev William Carr, Rector of Bolton Priory from 1799 to 1813, laid out 30 miles of footpaths in the Duke of Devonshire's woodlands, even providing seats at the best viewpoints for the hundreds of visitors who came to these idyllic landscapes, forerunners of the present thousands. But neither they nor the Devonshires who owned the land were likely to have referred to their woodlands as examples of 'amenity planting'. Like all who plant trees, they were thinking of future generations, a policy now being adopted in modern times by the National Park Authority.

Tree conservation

Trees are a traditional and valuable part of the Dales landscape. Not only do they contribute to the individuality of each dale but they are important wildlife habitats providing shelter and food for birds, animals and insects. Additionally, as farmers and landowners appreciate, trees and woods give shelter to grazing stock, especially during the winter. Yet only about 2 per cent of the National Park area is wooded, half of this by remnants of old woodland, half by coniferous woods planted this century to yield timber. The Dales no longer have to produce timber for building or for fuel, and over the years a tradition of tree and woodland management has largely disappeared. To redress the balance by positive action the National Park Authority places tree planting high on its list of priorities. It is carried out either directly by the Authority or through management grants (to which reference has already been made).

Native or traditional trees are planted, usually a mixture of oak, ash, rowan, hawthorn and alder, and it is mainly farmers who are interested in these grant-aid schemes to improve their land, provide shelter for stock and eventually yield usable timber. To fence a 100ft (30m) square plot enclosing 200 young trees and provide rabbit-guards – tall slim plastic cylinders – costs about £550, of which the Authority will contribute £500.

A different type of woodland management is now being practised near Aysgarth Falls in Wensleydale. The National Park Authority recently bought the 30 acre (12ha) Freeholders' Wood on the north side of the river, an ancient coppiced hazel wood with common rights long enjoyed by twenty-nine householders of Carperby. The wood has been a rich and colourful habitat for wildlife, but pressure by thousands of visitors seeking access to, and viewpoints of, the middle and lower falls, has caused much concern to the Authority. Now that they own it, they are in a position to exercise control over its use and improve the footpaths through it. With the approval of the Freeholders it is intended to manage the woodland and to reintroduce the system of coppicing.

The wood has been divided into blocks of about an acre (0.4ha) and each year two such blocks will have their trees felled to stump level, but leaving one standard tree in every twelve untouched as in former coppicing. When broad-leaved trees are thus felled, new shoots grow from the 'stool', and in eighteen years' time these will be ready for cutting again. Thus, over an eighteen-year cycle there will be a changing pattern of light and shade, encouraging an increase in the variety of all

Coppiced hazel in
Freeholders' Wood,
Carperby, Wensleydale –
now owned by
the National Park

forms of flora and fauna, especially the flowers. More importantly this ancient woodland will survive and flourish for generations to come. At its eastern end a small area of land was recently planted with over three hundred native trees which, it is hoped, will eventually grow into an attractive copse.

Here, as in most broad-leaved woodlands of the Dales, good cover encourages many species of nesting birds. These include blackbirds, thrushes, chaffinches, blue tits, wood warblers, garden warblers, as well as green and greater-spotted woodpeckers, and woodpigeons. Rooks and jackdaws favour shelter-belts and scar woods.

Most woodlands have one or two resident pairs of grey squirrels, and higher-level woods are favourite places for foxes' earths. Badgers are widely if thinly scattered about the Dales, but, like foxes, being nocturnal creatures, are rarely seen. Observant walkers may identify their regular tracks from setts to feeding areas, but no great powers of observation are needed to recognise that rabbits are apparently thriving. Large colonies inhabit extensive warrens, particularly in the friable shale slopes beneath limestone scars in the northern dales, and it is noticeable that many rabbits seem to be favouring holes burrowed in the lower courses of stone walls. Myxomatosis may be keeping numbers in check, but roadside casualties are probably no less responsible for controlling the rabbit population. Hedgehogs, too, are frequent victims of motor vehicles, and few journeys in the Dales are without a sighting of crows or black-headed gulls enjoying a meal from last night's accident victims.

Brown hares, restricting their activities to upland pastures remote from roads, have few enemies other than local packs of beagles, and maintain their numbers well. Far more unpopular, and probably far less frequently seen, are wild mink, which, escaping from fur farms, started to breed on the Yorkshire–Lancashire border about twenty years ago and are now quite numerous along some Dales rivers, especially the Nidd, Wharfe and Ribble, as well as in Wensleydale.

In any microcosm of the Dales landscape, conservation means change. In any living environment this must be expected, for neither life nor the conditions which sustain it are static. Man is almost certainly the greatest cause of change, as well as of destruction. It is one of his more unfortunate habits to draw attention to what is special and, by so doing, increase the threat of its extinction by encouraging others to come to see it. But most of the non-human life of the Yorkshire Dales is ordinary enough to be simply taken for granted. A wider understanding of it would help to ensure that it is not harmed through ignorance.

8
EXPLORING THE DALES

A survey made in the mid-1970s showed that on a typical summer Sunday 75,000 visitors entered the National Park seeking recreation, and at peak periods at least 7,000 cars would be parked within the Park area. It is probable that these figures have marginally increased in the years since then. Of the visitors 48 per cent were on holiday trips, 57 per cent on day visits from their homes. Any change in these percentages has probably only been slight; I suspect there has been an increase in the proportion of holiday visitors at the expense of day visitors. Certainly there has been a significant increase in accommodation for visitors, particularly in the provision of holiday cottages for rent.

When National Parks were first designated thirty years ago it was envisaged that the people who used them would be participants in active recreation – walking, climbing, cycling, canoeing, bird-watching, etc. The motor-car explosion has changed the picture, so that, in most National Parks, sightseeing by car has become the accepted norm. In the mid-1970s, it was expected, for example, that of all visitors to the Yorkshire Dales only between 8 per cent and 10 per cent were likely to take walks of more than 2 miles. Recent evidence suggests that a higher proportion of visitors now like to explore the Park on foot, even if they have arrived at their starting-point by car. Perhaps this is the result of improvements in signposting or waymarking, as well as the maintenance in good order of a network of public footpaths extending over 1,000 miles. Perhaps it is the burgeoning library of useful literature on the subject, perhaps the increasing influence of the National Park

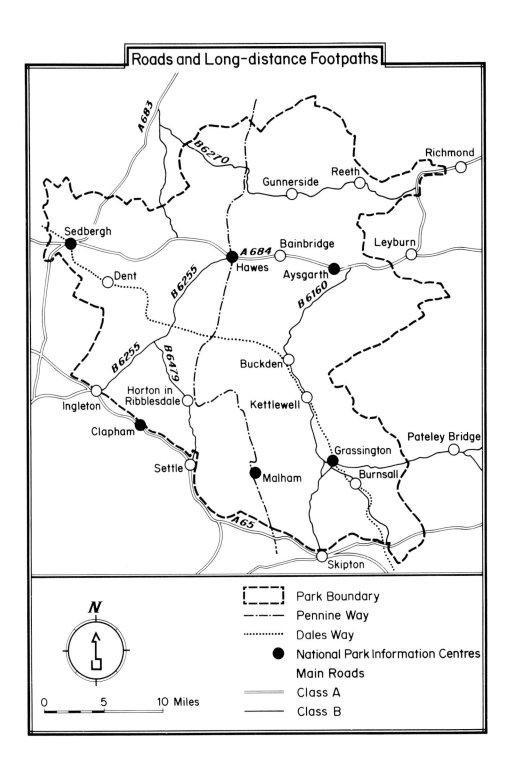

Roads and Long-distance Footpaths

Richmond

A683

B6270

Reeth

Gunnerside

Sedbergh

Bainbridge

Leyburn

Dent

A684

Hawes

Aysgarth

B6255

B6160

B6255

B6479

Buckden

Horton in Ribblesdale

Kettlewell

Ingleton

Pateley Bridge

Clapham

Grassington

Settle

Burnsall

Malham

A65

Skipton

N

0   5   10 Miles

- - - - Park Boundary
- · - · - Pennine Way
·········· Dales Way
● National Park Information Centres
Main Roads
═══ Class A
─── Class B

Committee's programme of over 110 guided walks during a normal holiday season. In any event, this chapter is concerned mainly with the motorist sightseer and the walker, while the cyclist should also find plenty that is of relevance.

Motor tours in the Dales

All explorers in the Dales travel, for the most part, along old roads and tracks. Motorists on the busy A65 along the Park's southern edge are using a route probably dating from prehistoric times, although its present course largely follows the line of the Keighley–Kendal turnpike of 1753, modified between Long Preston and Settle seventy years later. The road up the eastern side of Wharfedale from Grassington to Kettlewell, then climbing over Park Rash into Coverdale, and finally to Middleham, is part of the London–Barnsley–Richmond road surveyed by Ogilby in 1675. The Richmond–Redmire–Askrigg–Bainbridge road is part of the original turnpike of 1751, while the present A684 from Bainbridge into Hawes, and the B6277 to Ribble Head are its 1795 improvement. Small, winding, minor roads between villages may have evolved from inter-village tracks of the Anglian settlement; indeed, evolution is the method by which most roads in the Dales have arrived at their present state. Even the turnpike roads were mainly improvements to existing ones. The only roads deliberately created were the few Roman ones already mentioned.

Two further points for motorists. Garages and petrol pumps are few in the upper parts of the main valleys. Arkengarthdale, Bishopdale, Coverdale and Littondale have none, so it is as well to ensure you are well 'topped-up' before making long journeys. From a driving point of view, there are few main roads, and the only Category I trunk road, the A65, keeps to the southern margin of the Park. Except for the A684 through Wensleydale and Garsdale most valley roads are narrow, although the B6255 Hawes–Ingleton, the B6479 Settle–Horton, and the B6160 Grassington–Skipton have been widened and straightened to accommodate quarry traffic. Not only are other roads narrow and winding, but small verges and adjoining stone walls create problems if wide vehicles are encountered. Walls themselves are sometimes so high that they restrict forward visibility where bends occur, so the advice is to drive with care. Roads which cross watersheds are usually unenclosed over the high moors and fells, often with wide grass sward at the roadside inviting visitors to park and enjoy the view. When driving along these routes be prepared for sheep to cross the road in front of you.

In pastoral country stock are frequently on the move, either of their own accord or driven – when they are moved from one field to another, for example, or collected for market. From April to October, they are moved twice daily for milking; 8–9.30am and 4.30–6.00pm are the most likely times to be delayed by a herd of cows. There is no point in hooting or trying to hurry past, for cows cannot be hurried. It is far wiser to be patient.

The tours suggested are of various lengths between 30 and 80 miles. The qualities of landscape, scenery, buildings and villages are the criteria, not mileage. Each is a circular tour, starting and finishing at one or other of the more popular holiday centres, although obviously other starting-points can be used where they are more convenient. The Landranger maps, which are to a scale of 1:50,000, are more useful than motoring maps, and Sheet 98 (Wensleydale and Wharfedale) covers about 90 per cent of the National Park area.

1 Reeth–Swaledale–Arkengarthdale–Reeth

This tour takes in the austere beauty of the northernmost valleys in the Park linked by a few miles of wilderness landscape either side of Tan Hill Inn. Take the road westwards up Swaledale, with recommended stops at Gunnerside, Muker and Keld, particularly to appreciate the wonderful pattern of stone barns and walled fields. To enjoy riverside scenery you will have to walk at Muker and Keld. Half a mile beyond the village turn right, and after a short, steep climb with two hairpin bends to West Stonesdale, drive through wild, moorland scenery to Tan Hill Inn, with the Pennine Way taking a parallel course a quarter of a mile to the east. Turn right at Tan Hill, ie eastwards to Arkengarthdale, reaching after 4 miles the first farms and their enclosed fields, and the melancholy beauty of former lead-mining landscapes. Choose at CB whether to continue down the valley to Reeth or to cross the watershed southwards to Swaledale. This moorland road takes you past the 'Herriot' watersplash and Surrender Bridge (there is good parking at both), where a track leads to the famous lead-mining complex at Old Gang.

2 Leyburn–Middleham–Coverham–Coverdale–Kettlewell–Buckden–Bishopdale–Thoralby–West Burton–Leyburn

This tour takes in four valleys Wensleydale, Coverdale, Wharfedale and Bishopdale, a former royal castle (Middleham), the tranquility of a small monastic ruin, and Coverdale's remote grandeur, followed by the steep descent of Park Rash into Kettlewell and Wharfedale. Then return across the watershed by Kidstones Pass into Bishopdale with its wealth of seventeenth-century farmhouses. Below Street Head Inn make a short detour to Thoralby to see more fine vernacular buildings, and to West Burton to enjoy its village green and nearby waterfall, before joining the A684, through Swinithwaite and West Witton (more fine houses) to Wensley (church) and Leyburn.

3 Leyburn–Redmire–Castle Bolton–Carperby–Aysgarth–Askrigg–Oxnop –Swaledale–Grinton–Bellerby–Leyburn

This is a tour revealing village variety, with interesting houses at Redmire, the forbidding castle of the Scropes and the village of Castle Bolton which served it. Note the strip lynchets (see Chapter 3) above the road between Bolton and Carperby. Turn down to Aysgarth (National Park Centre and carpark) for its waterfalls and woodlands. Continue along Wensleydale's northern side, past Nappa Hall, to Askrigg, where there are eighteenth-century houses, a cross, the house filmed as the home of TV's Yorkshire vet, a church and a walk to waterfalls, in Whitfield Gill. From Askrigg turn up the moor road, keeping left, over Askrigg Common, past Oxnop Scar, and fine views

Oxnop, a wild pass between Swaledale and Wensleydale. Oxnop Scar, on the right, is formed of the Main Limestone at the top of the Yoredale series of strata

before descent to Swaledale. Turn down Swaledale to Grinton, right (south) up the hill, keep left past Grinton Lodge (youth hostel), past lead-mining remains above Cogden Beck, to Bellerby crossroads, Bellerby and Leyburn.

4 Hawes–Thwaite–Keld–Nateby–Pendragon–Moorcock–Hawes

This tour shows Pennine contrasts around the headwaters of three rivers – the Swale, Eden and Ure. Take the Buttertubs Pass to upper Swaledale, pausing at the Buttertubs themselves, which are remarkable limestone potholes by the roadside. There are splendid views as you descend to Thwaite, and pastoral landscapes to Keld. Take the wild road to the head of Swaledale, past riverside limestone scars and limekilns to the high commons above Mallerstang, enjoying superb views over the Vale of Eden from Tailrigg, before the long descent to Nateby. Turn left up Mallerstang, pausing at Pendragon Castle, before making the long easy climb to Aisgill at the summit of the Settle–Carlisle Railway, then down to the Moorcock Inn and east to Hawes.

5 Hawes–Semerwater–Bainbridge–Aysgarth–Bishopdale–Buckden–Hubberholme–Langstrothdale–Hawes

This tour takes in important landscape features and fine examples of vernacular buildings. Take the A684 eastwards from Hawes. After a mile turn right to Burtersett, then pass the nineteenth-century stone-mine workings on the hillside to the south. Climb to cross the Roman road, and go round the hill to Countersett, noting its seventeenth-century Hall and nearby Friends' meeting-house. Then there is a view of, and descent to, Semerwater, along its northern shore; then turn sharp left, past good farmhouses before the descent to Bainbridge with its fine green, stocks, houses and Low Mill. Rejoin the main road eastwards to Aysgarth. Divert left at Worton to see Worton Hall, built in 1600. Between Worton and Aysgarth many excellent examples of drumlins (rounded hills) and eskers (low, elongated mounds) are seen on both sides of the road. These have been formed by the action of glaciers. Pause at Aysgarth church, with its fifteenth-century screens from Jervaulx Abbey. Visit Aysgarth Falls if desired.

Turn south for Thoralby or West Burton (or both – see Tour 2) and drive up Bishopdale. Note West New House to the west near the head of the valley before crossing the watershed by Kidstones Pass and the descent to Buckden. Turn up Wharfedale to Hubberholme (church), Yockenthwaite (farm groups, pack-horse bridge, stone circle across river). There is riverside scenery of great charm, with roadside parking,

Bainbridge in Wensleydale, looking west from the Roman fort on Brough Hill

up Langstrothdale. Beyond Oughtershaw climb to Fleet Moss, York-shire's highest road, noticing the changes in colours from the limestone valley to the gritstone moors. Cross the Roman road just before the steep descent to Duerley and the village of Gayle. Look around Gayle – there is a good variety of houses both sides of the beck. Return to Hawes.

6 *Hawes–Garsdale–Sedbergh–Dent–Newby Head–Hawes*

This tour shows valley and river contrasts, the effects of afforestation, and open views at the head of Wensleydale. Take the A684 west from Hawes, through Appersett, and note the tree planting at Thwaite Bridge and the change of valley scenery west of the Moorcock Inn as the road threads the narrow trough of Garsdale, with farms and barns regularly dispersed along the lower hillsides. A roadside carpark on un-enclosed Longstone Fell affords magnificent views of the Howgill Fells. Below, the River Clough enters an impressive gorge, where the Sedgwick geology trail invites exploration.

Turn left in Sedbergh for Dentdale, where hedges, not walls, are the usual field boundaries. High above the south side of the valley Combe

Scar represents the results of ice-action scooping out a huge hollow below tall cliffs, a landscape feature rare in the Yorkshire Dales. Burton Hill (673898), reached on foot along a farm track, but not visible from the road, is one of the best seventeenth-century farmhouses in Dent-dale. The good, scenic carpark in Dent encourages exploration of the most unusual village in the National Park. Eastwards from Dent the better road crosses the river and keeps to the north side of the valley, passing more good farmhouses, mostly whitewashed.

At Lea Yeat, keep right and follow the upper valley southwards. Pause near Stone House (very narrow bridge) and observe the water-worn nature of the river-bed, and the old pack-horse track behind Stone House, beneath Arten Gill viaduct. The road climbs out of the valley, under Dent Head viaduct (look for the unusual pack-horse bridge beneath an arch). Beyond, good views to the north show the Settle–Carlisle line. Turn left at the next road junction, pass Newby Head, a former drovers' inn, now one of the highest farms in the Dales. On the journey down Widdale to Hawes, notice the maturing conifer plantations, dating from the late 1960s.

7 *Sedbergh–River Rawthey–Pendragon Castle–Mallerstang–Garsdale–Sedbergh*
Although this tour goes outside the National Park, its rewards are fine views of the Howgill Fells. Take the A683 Kirkby Stephen road, prefer-ably in the morning, when sunlight models the Howgills' eastern flanks. Cautley Spout can be seen from the roadside, but is better ap-preciated in the closer view obtained by walkers. There is a very good view from the minor road beyond Rawthey Bridge, which rejoins the A683 in 3 miles, and in another 3 miles turn right across Wharton Fell (mainly unenclosed common, with wide-ranging views). This road descends to Pendragon Castle and joins the road up Mallerstang (see Tour 4), to the Moorcock. Turn right, and follow the A684 to Sedbergh (see Tour 6).

8 *Settle–Ribble Head–Ingleton–Settle*
A 30 mile circuit of Ingleborough, with limestone scenery all the way. You will want to make plenty of stops! Follow the B6479 northwards up Ribblesdale, detouring into Langcliffe and Stainforth to enjoy their contrasts – one with a green, the other a compact cluster with a beck through the middle. Stainforth pack-horse bridge is to the west of the

Cautley Crags and the Cross Keys Inn, Howgill Fells, near Sedbergh

main road and worth seeing. There is a carpark at Horton, so explore the village, church and Pennine Way, and muse on the effects of modern quarrying. At Selside, park in the lane north of the hamlet, to appreciate the farmhouses and barns. Beyond on the right is the most extensive area of drumlins in the Dales. Ribble Head invites a longer stop, at the heart of the Three Peaks country – Whernside to the west, Ingleborough to the south-west, and Penyghent more distant, to the south-east. You may wonder why people climb them or – worse – cycle up them. Immediate interests at Ribble Head are the river, the limestone caves and the many low limestone scars. Be adventurous! Walk across and see them, as they are the most accessible in the Dales. This is the area where you learn about limestone, and love it or hate it, but cannot ignore it. If you are lucky, a train might add character to the great Ribble Head viaduct while you are there.

Follow the B6255 south-west to Ingleton The carpark at Chapel-le-Dale is a starting-point for one way up Ingleborough or, much closer, Souther Scales pavement (nature reserve). Between Chapel-le-Dale and Ingleton limestone scars etch the hillsides and, near Ingleton, the entrance to White Scar Caves is passed. Ingleton merits a long stay, especially if the Falls Walk is to be enjoyed (see Chapter 1).

The third leg of the triangle, along Ingleborough's southern flanks, is best enjoyed by taking the old road which leaves the village just above the police station, signposted Clapham. Divert at Newby for a brief look round this attractive little village, but allow plenty of time for a prolonged stop at Clapham, using the large carpark by the information centre (see Gazetteer for details). After Clapham, join the A65 for a mile but then divert to Austwick, where the Norber boulders should be visited. Rejoin the main road which, in 2 miles, reaches Buckhaw Brow, with Giggleswick Scars on the left. This is the classic view along the line of the Mid Craven Fault. Another short diversion, into Giggleswick, to see its church and good village houses, is an appropriate climax to the journey.

9 *Settle–Stainforth–Littondale–Malham–Settle*

This is a circuit of the Craven uplands, past green pastures, white limestone crags and walls, and charming villages. Leave the B6479 Ribble Head road at Stainforth, and climb northwards into Silverdale, with Penyghent ahead. Continue past Hesleden and descend to Halton Gill at the head of Littondale. Drive down this lovely valley through Litton to Arncliffe, and turn right (signposted Malham) to climb steeply out of the village, with Cowside Beck far below and Yew Cogar Scar above it. Continue past Darnbrook House (gate across road) and Tennant Gill to join the Malham road at a crossroads west of Malham Tarn. Turn left (east) along the road known as the 'Streets', noticing the stumpy remains of the smelt-mill chimney on the right. After a mile (National Trust signs) unenclosed land encourages parking, for there is much to explore around here, but only on foot.

Malham Tarn is ¼ mile north; the Pennine Way runs northwards towards Tarn House, and a track southwards leads to Water Sinks and the famous Dry Valley at Watlowes, continuing to the top of Malham Cove. The road goes eastwards to Street Gate, continuing beyond as a green road, Mastiles Lane. The metalled road swings south and descends steeply to Malham village. Below the fourth bend a footpath on the right (ladder stile) provides the shortest, easiest approach to the pavement at the top of Malham Cove. For the low-level approach and for exploring the village, use the large carpark at the information centre. Continue southwards to Kirkby Malham (village and church), turn right and climb to Scosthrop Moor (good view south), past Scaleber Bridge (841626) and a waterfall, and into Upper Settle. Half a mile west of Scaleber Bridge, a bridleway and footpath on the right offer the best approach to Attermire Scars.

10 *Grassington–Bolton Abbey–Skipton–Gargrave–Malham–Littondale–Grassington*

This tour offers the pastoral scenery of lower Wharfedale by the Bolton Priory ruins, then a busy market town, then parkland – white limestone crags and scars, and attractive villages. Many narrow, winding roads. Take the Threshfield, then Burnsall, roads out of Grassington. Divert to Linton to see this beautiful village. Burnsall deserves a stop, for the church, school and river scenery. Beyond, the route passes Barden Tower before reaching Bolton Abbey. Allow plenty of time for these serene priory ruins in a glorious riverside setting. There are miles of walks near-by, including Strid Woods Nature Trail. Turn right on to the minor road to Halton and Embsay for a more scenic route to Skipton.

Join the A59 to Gargrave, then minor roads northwards via Eshton, Airton and Kirkby Malham, to Malham. Note lynchets (see Chapter 3) and walled fields on the approach to Malham. Route details from Malham are the reverse of those in the second part of Tour 9. Follow the signposts for Arncliffe, and there take the road down the south side of Littondale, joining Wharfedale at Skirfare Bridge and passing Kilnsey Crag after half a mile. Turn left, and cross the river to Conis-

Burnsall Morris Men in the square at Grassington

tone, a village of splendid houses and barns. Take the minor road southwards down Wharfedale, passing the lower part of Grass Wood (nature reserve) and entering Grassington at the crossroads below its main street.

Walks in the Dales

Three OS Outdoor Leisure maps, on the scale of $2\frac{1}{2}$ in to the mile (or 1:25,000), are the best guide for walkers. The sheet entitled 'Yorkshire Dales: Northern and Central Area' covers Arkengarthdale, Swaledale, Wensleydale and Wharfedale above Kettlewell. 'Yorkshire Dales: Southern Area' covers Wharfedale below Kettlewell, extending southwards to Skipton and westwards to Ribblesdale as far as Horton; i.e. most of the Craven country including Malham. 'Yorkshire Dales: Western Area' overlaps this and the first map, on its eastern edge, by including Ribblesdale above Settle and Wensleydale west of Hawes. This map includes the Three Peaks, Garsdale and Dentdale, but excludes the north-west corner of the National Park. All public rights-of-way are clearly shown – footpaths, bridleways and the long-distance paths (which are indicated by special symbols). Information provided on the maps also includes all field boundaries and local features, so that such maps simplify the planning of walks even if their size makes them a bit unwieldy on an open hillside in a high wind! As evocations of pleasure, both in anticipation and in retrospect, they are unbeatable.

Special footpath maps, also on the 1:25,000 scale, covering smaller local areas are also available, from information centres and local shops, and are excellent value for money. Most popular localities are covered. Additionally, the National Park Committee has published a series of 'walk-cards', which detail individual walks and highlight points of interest, to help visitors to enjoy self-guided walks.

While many paths are identified by signposts and yellow waymarks, and many bridleways by blue markers, many others lack such identification, mainly because some farmers and landowners have not given permission for waymarking. Thus, while you *know* you have a right to use a waymarked track, the absence of waymarking does *not* imply there is *no* right-of-way. If the OS map indicates a right-of-way, even though it may not be apparent on the ground, it does exist and you can use it. In so doing you should recognise that many public paths cross meadows and pastures where important hay crops are critical to the farming economy. It is therefore essential that in using paths which cross such fields you keep in single file to reduce unnecessary damage to mowing grass.

Gates should be left as you find them, which usually means closed. Wandering stock can become mixed with others, mate prematurely, upset cropping regimes, stray on to the roads or even cause a spread of infection. Courteous behaviour to farmers and landowners costs nothing; its rewards are for the people who follow you. The law now allows farmers to graze some breeds of beef bulls with cows or heifers in fields crossed by rights-of-way. It is advisable always to give them a wide berth and not to provoke them. Dairy bulls, usually black and white Friesians, should not be grazed where there are public paths, and in any case should be avoided. Young bullocks are invariably curious about humans and will frequently come towards you, but will do nothing more than that, unless provoked. If you walk with a dog, keep it under control, preferably visibly on a lead. This goes some way to reassuring farmers that you are a responsible and thoughtful person.

A similar attitude of common sense should apply to your clothing. It should be comfortable and practical, particularly so far as footwear is concerned. Walking boots are best, not climbing boots, which may be too heavy. Boots give protection to ankles, which can easily be sprained, especially in descending steep or rough slopes. 'Commando' or 'Vibram' soles help to give a good grip, especially on wet grass.

Strong shoes or even 'trainers' are suitable for straightforward field or riverside paths, but not for fell-walking, and if you expect to be walking on the 'tops', a compass is advisable. It helps navigation in mist and low cloud, provided you know how to use it in conjunction with a map. But common sense is the best guide; if weather conditions are bad, or forecasts suggest they could become bad, there is little point in seeking trouble. Good, low-level walks abound.

Many walkers' tracks are deliberate creations. Britain's first long-distance footpath, the Pennine Way, a bright gleam in Tom Stephenson's eye in the 1930s, was designated in 1951 but not officially opened until 1965, at a ceremony which took place at Malham. Now, thousands of walkers each year plod its course for 250 miles from Derbyshire to the Scottish border. There is no doubt that some of its most memorable and scenic stretches are in the Dales. Within the National Park it covers about 55 miles from Gargrave to Tan Hill, taking in all types of Pennine landscape on the way. Other long-distance paths, official or unofficial, are the Dales Way from Ilkley to Bowness in the Lake District, the Coast-to-Coast walk evolved by A. Wainwright, which in its Dales section follows Swaledale's northern watershed, the Yoredale Way in Wensleydale, the recently established Ribblesdale Way, and, east of the Park, the Nidderdale Way. While most of these link existing rights-of-way, some new sections have been created by negotiation with farmers and landowners. Some of the most pleasant paths are the old ones around the villages, and the pack-horse tracks and drove roads crossing the lonely fells. The dozen walks described represent a good cross-section of what the Dales can offer.

1 *Upper Swaledale (7½ miles)*
Riverside, woodland and a high-level limestone shelf combine to provide one of the most superb walks in the Dales. This route starts and finishes at Muker, but it could be Thwaite or Keld.

Take the field paths (signposted Keld) north from the village and go through a succession of hay-meadows. Cross the river by a footbridge and take the broad track up the eastern side of the valley. Cross the beck at the foot of Swinnergill, by the ruins of Beldi smelt-mill, and climb towards Crackpot Hall, passing below the ruins of a farm. The path continues west, high above the river gorge, with impressive views. Eventually, it descends to a footbridge across East Gill (Pennine Way *and* Coast-to-Coast path sign); turn left and cross the river by a footbridge; go up a short steep track and then turn sharp left along the Pennine Way (unless you want to visit Keld, ¼ mile ahead).

Follow good tracks through woodland, climbing intermittently, and continue to follow the Pennine Way signs until the open hillside is reached. The track now levels out along a stony limestone terrace on the north flank of Kisdon, with the River Swale far below. Continue for a mile, swinging westwards and descending to some barns and a house. A walled lane descends steeply from near here, providing a quick return to Muker. The full walk continues along the Pennine Way, behind Kisdon Farm, and descends across a heather-bracken hillside to Thwaite. Turn left before the village and take field paths towards Muker, joining the road west of the village.

2 Gunnerside Gill (5 miles)

This walk offers the quintessence of lead-mining landscapes in a wild, austerely beautiful valley. It starts and finishes in Gunnerside village.

Follow the signposts for Gunnerside Gill, along the path by the east side of the beck. Walk for a mile, by the beck, through woods and across pastures, before the wilder landscape is revealed ahead, with old levels, dressing-floors and an increasing number of spoil-heaps. The path climbs the hillside along pack-horse tracks to Bunton Level amid savage, hush-riven scenery. Continue beyond Bunton's ruined buildings and descend to the beck, for the last half a mile to Blakethwaite Mill and peat store.

Retrace your steps to Bunton, and continue south on your original route for another ¼ mile, then take the grassy track leading up the hillside to the left, through bracken, levelling-out near an impressive limekiln below Winterings Edge. Follow a grassy track south, gradually losing height as it approaches a few widely scattered former farms, now holiday cottages. The track winds past them, swings north above a small, steep valley, then hairpins back on itself and descends steeply into Lodge Green at the eastern end of Gunnerside village.

3 Riverside Ramble (about 2 miles)

Based on Reeth, this walk offers gentle walking through riverside scenery, and pleasant open views.

Leave Reeth Green on the south side between the Congregational church and the Literary Institute. Go along Back Lane and bear left at the fork. At the signpost take the path indicated 'Harkerside and Grinton', which leads directly to the suspension bridge across the river. Cross this and follow the riverside path to the left. Excellent views back to the north and north-west show a variety of field systems including medieval strip lynchets (see Chapter 3) and early nineteenth-century enclosures. Beyond Reeth, the limestone scar of Fremington Edge includes lead-mine spoil-heaps.

Keep straight ahead where the river leaves the path and loops northwards. After ½ mile the path joins a minor road near Swale Hall (seventeenth-century house) and reaches Grinton church in another ¼ mile. Go through the churchyard, leave it at the east end, turn left on the road, cross Grinton bridge and take the footpath on the left immediately after, crossing meadows and aiming for Fremington Mill. On reaching the road turn left, cross Arkle Beck and enter Reeth at the foot of the green.

4 *Lower Bishopdale (5 miles)*

This is an easy walk with rewarding views, based on West Burton.

Leave the bottom of the village along the Leyburn road, and almost immediately cross Burton Bridge (pack-horse) and walk along a walled, metalled lane past Flanders Hall (1779). At the top of the first wood, where the rough road climbs up to the right, go through a field gate on the left, following a field path above a scar wood on the left, maintaining the same height for a mile. There is a small heronry in the wood to the left; then two of the follies in Sorrelsykes Park can be glimpsed. The path eventually leaves the woodland and swings towards Temple Farm at the main road. Turn right (signposted 'Templars' Chapel') and fol-

Wensleydale, looking across to Bishopdale from above Redmire. The scattered broad-leaved trees contribute to the beauty of this scene

low the track up to a scar wood; climb steeply through it to emerge by the ruins (footings only) of an early-thirteenth-century chapel of the Knights Templars, a military order under strict religious rule. Continue across a field, and turn right to the next scar wood, reaching a concrete farm track, which turns right, still climbing. Go ahead (southwards) up the lower flanks of Pen Hill, to a walled lane running east–west. Turn right and follow this lane, which widens into a fine green road, probably used by the Lords of Middleham to reach their hunting forest of Bishopdale Chase and later used by pack-horses and drovers.

Continue to Morpeth Scar, with magnificent views up Bishopdale and Wensleydale. The quick way to West Burton keeps to this track as it descends Morpeth Gate to Burton Bridge. The better way is to keep left, contouring above the scar, noticing how the wall changes from limestone to sandstone. Continue for half a mile, past four boundary walls on the right; then turn down a field path (signposted West Burton) which drops steeply across the contours as it heads directly for the village below.

5 Aysgarth–Carperby–Ox Close–Disher Force–Aysgarth (5½ miles)

Mainly field paths, visiting an old stone mine, a lead mine and a prehistoric circle, this walk always provides good views over Wensleydale. It starts and finishes at the National Park carpark at Aysgarth.

Walk up the road from the carpark. At the top of the wood turn right through a gate into Freeholders' Wood, and after a hundred yards look for a stone squeezer stile in the wall on the left. This and the next six stiles are all waymarked, and the path goes through a succession of fields to Carperby. Note the walling, which includes field-clearance or river boulders (rounded) and quarried stones (sharper edged). Turn right in the village, and after a hundred yards go left up Peat Moor Lane for half a mile. Before this track starts to climb, go left through a gate and follow the track below the scar. This levels out at the dressing-floor of Carperby Stone Mine, worked in the last century. Note the piles of flagstones and the cave-like opening of the mine at the foot of a sandstone outcrop. Above the sandstone is the limestone scar, a nice example of a cyclothem within the Yoredale Series.

Continue westwards on a grassy track, through a gate in a long boundary wall, on to Ox Close, the large common field where oxen were grazed. Within a quarter of a mile the good grassy track passes, on the right, two Bronze Age stone circles, the second larger and more evident than the first. Ahead, to the right, rough cliffs and scattered spoil-heaps mark the former Wet Groves lead-mine, which worked from c1750 until c1880. Careful searching reveals fragments of lead-ore, and plenty of calcite, fluorite and barytes.

Continue westwards until Disher Force is reached. Turn left by the fall and follow the track down, past more workings, until it levels out and heads eastwards towards Ballowfield carpark. Keep north of the beck and climb through an old, coppiced hazel and birch wood, observing the magnificent drumlin of Lady Hill, pine-crowned, across the road to the right. Follow the field path, going over a succession of stone stiles, to Carperby football field. Cross to the road, and follow the Aysgarth road back to the carpark. In a quarter of a mile, a waymarked stile on the right indicates a path across Bear Park which may be preferred to the road and leads to the west end of the carpark.

6 Askrigg–Mill Gill–Whitfield Gill–Askrigg (maximum 3 miles)

This is a short walk of outstanding geological interest, with two fine waterfalls in a gill wood.

The path leaves the village along West End, north of the church, and at the end of the road is signposted Mill Gill. It crosses the beck and climbs the west side of the gill. Make a short diversion to view Mill Gill Force, before leaving the wood for a field path west along Spen Rigg. Go through fields to a walled road, and turn right to the group of three houses at Helm, passing in front of them. Climb the pasture to a new path which gives access to Whitfield Gill, crossing the beck by a footbridge and climbing steeply up the east side of the gill. Near the top is a dramatic view of Whitfield Force. The path emerges high above it, to the right, on to a walled lane called Low Straights. Follow this eastwards to Askrigg Moor Road (which crosses to Swaledale), returning to the village down the hill. Alternatively, where the lane crosses a small ford, the field path on the right offers a pleasanter return route.

7 Hubberholme–Cray–Hubberholme (3 miles)

This is a gem of a walk, full of quiet, pastoral beauty, in upper Wharfedale, based on Hubberholme. Park by the church.

Take the field gate to the right of the churchyard, taking the rough farm track behind the church to Scar House, passing close to the house with its date stones (1698 and 1876). Turn right between the house and barn, then up a rough, stony track to a signpost for Cray, Hubberholme and Yockenthwaite. Turn right and follow a level track on soft, springy turf eastwards above Hubberholme Wood – a typical native woodland with ash, wych elm, hazel, holly and blackthorn. The view gradually widens out to reveal the glacier-smoothed floor of Wharfedale. Pass an area of limestone pavement on the right before crossing Crook Gill by a small footbridge. The track continues to the hamlet of Cray, where the White Lion offers bar snacks and morning coffee. There is no need to go as far as Cray, since the return route cuts back by the first (or last) cottage in the hamlet, descending south-westwards, parallel to some power lines, to join the west bank of Cray Gill. Cross an old pack-horse bridge and gradually lose height, enjoying idyllic scenery of waterfalls, cascades, wild flowers and trees. Joining the quiet road by the bridge at How Ings, turn right and return to Hubberholme church.

8 *Grassington–Lea Green–Conistone–Grass Wood–Grassington (7 miles)*
This walk traverses mainly upland limestone pasture, with sustained interest throughout.

Leave Grassington along Chapel Street, opposite the town hall. At Town Head Farm, pass behind the barn on the right, and go through fields, across three stiles, to a junction of tracks. Keep ahead, bearing slightly right, still northwards, with the wall in view to the right. Many sheep tracks, old field systems and old lead 'rakes' are seen on Lea Green, site of very old settlement. Keep ahead over good limestone turf, crossing four stiles, the second one a ladder stile. At the fourth stile a track comes in from the right, crossing the path diagonally. Turn left on to a north–west alignment, descending through an opening between scars into the gorge of Conistone Dib. Continue to Conistone village, turn left and left again at the southern end of the village (signposted to Grassington).

A track goes behind a farm and barn, gradually climbing towards limestone scars a mile ahead. At their end, veer left up a slope above another impressive wooded gorge, cross a stile, then bear right, and make a short, steep climb to another ladder stile. The path ahead across Lea Green is the shortest way back to Grassington. A better alternative is to turn right into the top of Bastow Wood, heading southeast to another ladder stile. Cross this and soon pick up a good track, through a woodland glade, working south-eastwards among the sylvan delights and wild flowers of Grass Wood. The path emerges and goes through a series of fields to Town Head at Grassington.

9 *Bolton Abbey–Strid Wood–Bolton Abbey (6 miles)*
Here you are offered riverside walking in the beautiful valley of lower Wharfedale, starting and finishing at the riverside carpark at Cavendish Pavilion.

Follow the west bank of the river through Strid Woods (a small toll is payable at the kiosk), preferably taking the upper path for its glorious views. The mature deciduous woodland is at its colourful best in autumn, and is scarcely less resplendent in late spring. The climax of this part of the walk is the Strid itself, where the River Wharfe surges with fearsome force through a narrow chasm of rocks, with potholes and whirlpools. Beyond the end of the wood cross the river by the aqueduct footbridge (permitted access), and turn right (east) to follow the riverside footpath along the left (north-east) bank, through more woodland. After a mile the track joins Hazlewood Lane near Posforth Bridge, and immediately past the bridge a path leads off to the right, re-joining the river bank and continuing in open country past the wooden footbridge spanning the river (which provides a short cut back to Cavendish Pavilion).

Rejoin the road briefly at Pickles Gill (ford and footbridge), and in fifty yards take a clear path on the right, which subsequently climbs to reward you with spectacular and memorable views of Bolton Priory, before descending to a sturdy footbridge and stepping-stones, by which you cross to the ruins, reaching the road to the north of these. Take the footpath above the river bank to the Cavendish Memorial and the riverside carpark.

10 Clapham–Long Lane–Thieves Moss–Crummackdale–Norber–Clapham (8 miles)

This walk provides superb limestone scenery and easy walking through-out. It starts and finishes at the National Park carpark at Clapham.

Walk up the village from the carpark, turning right along a lane at the church (signposted Austwick). Climb beneath tunnels, and at the end of the woods turn left (signposted Selside) into Long Lane, aptly named. There is a good view across Clapdale, and Ingleborough beyond. After 1½ miles emerge from the lane on to open upland. Follow a broad, grassy track up to the right, heading east-north-east. After about a mile this track meets another coming up from the south, with a good view of Penyghent's profile to the east. Continue northwards until the green track reaches a cross-wall at a gate, close to a wall on the right. Go through a small gate on the right, with Thieves Moss below and vast areas of limestone pavement all around. Descend to Thieves Moss and soon take a sketchy track threading a grassy route between the limestone outcrops, aiming for a small nick in the edge of the rocky plateau ahead. This is Beggar's Stile, which drops you down into the grassy pastures at the head of Crummackdale. Follow the broad green track southwards to the single farm at Crummack. It keeps above and to the west of the farm, becoming a distinct farm track beyond.

Continue down the Austwick road and past the entrance to Sowerthwaite Farm. Soon a stile on the right (signposted Norber) reveals a footpath leading to Nappa Scar, and a high stile beyond a small wood gives access to the open fell of Norber. Climb slightly to the right to see the extensive Norber erratics. Leave the boulder field by Robin Proctor's Scar on the south, where a path cuts down a rocky defile, heading south-westwards, skirting a former mere and joining the walled Thwaite Lane. Turn right and follow this back to Clapham.

11 *Around Dent (3 miles)*

This is a short, easy walk starting and finishing at the carpark in Dent.

Walk through the village, past the post office and Reading Room, and take a farm track on the right, crossing a cattle grid, passing a modern bungalow and climbing to Throstle Hall. Wide views open out behind you as you gain height. The way ahead lies south-eastwards across a field, then a series of field paths links scattered farms and their barns, with yellow waymarks identifying the route. West Banks, though derelict, is a good example of a seventeenth-century farmhouse.

The path continues above East Banks, and at East Helks descends to a concrete farm road in front of the house. A stile on the left near a barn takes the path diagonally over a field to the edge of a gill wood, crosses a footbridge, and as a narrow lane meets the Deepdale road at Coventree. Walk up this road to Slack, turn left at a stile opposite a cottage, and

Dent in Cumbria, from the north-east on a December morning

descend by a wall-side footpath to a road. Turn right, and in 300 yards, near Mill Bridge, turn sharp left on to a riverside path (signposted Church Bridge), following first Deepdale Beck and later the River Dee back to Dent. From Mill Bridge the route is that of the Dales Way.

12 *Malham–Janet's Foss–Gordale–Malham Cove–Malham* (*maximum 6 miles*)
This 'classic' walk in superb limestone country starts and finishes at the National Park carpark.

Follow the road towards the village. After 100yd cross Malham Beck on the right by a stone clapper bridge, and turn right on the opposite bank to join the Pennine Way through meadows for 300yd. Turn left along the path signposted 'Janet's Foss', following waymarks, past splendid barns and over ladder stiles. At New Laithe (notice the owl-hole in the barn's gable) the path enters woodland at a National Trust sign marked 'Little Gordale'. The track weaves through delightful woods, reaching Janet's Foss in a quarter of a mile. Beyond, it climbs over rocks into Gordale Lane. To see Gordale Scar at close range, turn right along the lane for 250yd, then left at the signpost for Gordale Scar. The foot of this unique gorge is 600yd away. Return to the road to where you originally joined it near Janet's Foss, and leave by a ladder stile on the right (signposted to Malham Cove).

Follow this path north-westwards, climbing towards the base of the Mid Craven Fault, through fields, behind the rounded hill of Cawden, a good example of a reef-knoll. Cross the Malham road at two ladder stiles, continuing across upland pasture to the limestone pavement above Malham Cove. To return directly to Malham, cross the pavement to a ladder stile at its western end, below which the Pennine Way descends by a long series of recently cut steps to a good path along the west side of the green valley, joining the road to the village.

The full walk leaves the Cove above its eastern end, taking the Pennine Way northwards along Trougate, originally a monastic track. This reaches the outlet stream from Malham Tarn at a ladder stile near the Water Sinks. Turn left and follow a path, grassy at first, soon very rocky, into a defile which becomes increasingly impressive, with Comb Scar on left. The track winds round and descends steeply into the famous dry valley of Watlowes. The 'Roman road' nature of the path is the result of recent footpath improvement by the National Park Authority. In about half a mile, this valley, formerly the surface course of Malham Water, suddenly emerges at the pavement of the Cove. From there, descend at its western end by the route described earlier.

GAZETTEER

An asterisk indicates that a place is given more detailed coverage in the main text.

Abbotside Almost 10,000 acres (4,000ha) of upland commons in Wensleydale, north of the river, extending eastwards from the Cumbria boundary almost to the Askrigg–Muker road. Roughly bisected by the Buttertubs Pass and the Pennine Way.

Airedale Upper part of the valley of the River Aire between Malham and Gargrave, so dominated by Malham that it is frequently known as Malhamdale. Dramatic limestone landscapes along the Mid Craven Fault, drumlins in the valley above Gargrave.

Airton Township in Kirkby Malham parish. Small triangular green with attractive houses round it. Linen-weaving replaced by cotton-spinning in eighteenth century. Former riverside mill now converted into flats. Pennine Way here takes a pleasant riverside path towards Malham.

Appletreewick Wharfedale village below Burnsall. Its lovely name means 'dairy farm near an apple tree'. Enjoyed medieval prosperity through lead-mining and subsequent sheep-farming under manorial ownership of Bolton Priory. Market charters and fair sustained village's importance until middle of last century. Stone houses line the main street between High Hall at the top and Low Hall at bottom. Between is the unusual Monk's Hall (1697), on site of a monastic grange. Glorious views, rewarding walks.

*Arkengarthdale Most northerly dale in the Park. Settlement pattern and names wholly Norse, landscape beautiful but melancholy with mining memories. Inviting moorland road traverses dale from Reeth, high above the Arkle Beck, continuing past Langthwaite and CB to Tan Hill, with a branch leading northwards over the Stang to Barnard Castle.

*Arncliffe Main village in Littondale, reached by minor roads from above Kilnsey or, more excitingly, from Malham. Ideally sited on well-drained gravels above River Skirfare, its cottages, houses, farms and barns front a spacious green. Behind the buildings are small, walled crofts; beyond them limestone walls soar to upland pastures above the scars. Charles Kingsley (1819–75), author of *The Water Babies* and *Westward Ho!*, frequently visited Bridge End, below the church, and across the river is Old Cotes (1650), a splendid yeoman's house.

*Askrigg Most important settlement in upper Wensleydale until Hawes (q.v.) usurped position after 1795. Main street gently winds and descends between prosperous houses and inns of eighteenth and early-nineteenth centuries, widening near parish church, where cobbles, cross and bull-ring evoke the past. Nearby is the 'Skeldale House' of James Herriot's TV vet in BBC series, now an Abbeyfield Home. Rev Malcolm Stonestreet's enterprise in 1970s resulted in the 'Askrigg Foundation' – revitalised local crafts, industries and community projects – but village heyday was really 1750–90, with trade benefitting from the Richmond–Lancaster turnpike through village. Askrigg's story, *Yorkshire Village* by M. Hartley and J. Ingilby is a classic of local history. Nearby Mill Gill and Whitfield Gill should not be missed.

Austwick Five miles north-west of Settle, and a good base for exploring the limestone country to north. A gentle village; some seventeenth-century houses with interesting lintels above their doorways.

*Aysgarth and Aysgarth Falls Village on main road up Wensleydale but has no great distinction other than a small green with stocks and an excellent pottery in a converted barn. Half a mile east, at Palmer Flatts, parish church stands in a huge churchyard. Steep hill descends to bridge with fine view of Upper Falls. National Park Centre and carpark on north side of valley: follow in famous footsteps of earlier travellers and tourists, by woodland paths to Middle and Lower Falls. They may not be Niagara, but after heavy rain are very impressive. Note coppicing in Freeholders' Wood, Yore Mills opposite (now the Yorkshire Museum of Carriages and Horse Drawn Vehicles), and John Carr's widening in 1784 of the old packhorse bridge. Field paths to nearby villages (Carperby, Thoralby and West Burton) were used by churchgoers, miners, millworkers and quarrymen. Castle Dykes on Aysgarth Moor, to south, probably of Bronze Age date, signifies long history of local settlement, but otherwise of limited interest.

*Bainbridge Attractive Wensleydale village with main road bisecting large rectangular green. All intimate views enclosed by eighteenth- and nineteenth-century houses. The '1443' on Rose and Crown not to be believed – there may have been an inn here in Tudor times, but the present frontage is Victorian! Low Mill, on north side of green, is a restored corn-mill with water-wheel and displays an unusual collection of dolls' houses. Climb Brough Hill to immediate north for best morning view of the village in its superb setting, probably not appreciated by the generations of Roman soldiery who occupied it in earlier times. River Bain, England's shortest river, has attractive falls above the bridge. On the Askrigg road the master's house of former Yorebridge School, c1840, is now one of the two National Park offices. The Beamish Reliability Run for old vehicles makes Bainbridge its southward limit and lunch-stop on the third Sunday in June.

Barbondale A narrow, wild, steep-sided valley south-west of Dent, threaded by a winding road that leads to the Lune valley and Kirkby Lonsdale. The Dent Fault lies along the line of the valley.

Barden The National Park Committee has arranged access agreements with the

Barden Bridge, Wharfedale, rebuilt 1676

Trustees of the Chatsworth Settlement whereby the public enjoy access over 14,000 acres (5,700ha) of Barden Fell, east of the Wharfe, and Barden Moor to the west and the use of specific paths leading to these areas. The areas may be closed on certain Saturdays and other weekdays in late summer, and also during times of high fire-risk. Dogs are prohibited at all times.

*Barden Tower   An impressive ruin in lower Wharfedale. The near-by, graceful, three-arched bridge, rebuilt in 1676, gives motorists access to minor road down east side of Wharfedale, as well as riverside carparking.

*Beamsley   A small village in lower Wharfedale famous for the strange, gritstone peak of Beamsley Beacon to its east, a superb viewpoint easily reached from the roadside above Langbar. Alongside the busy A59, Beamsley Hospital, founded in 1593, altered and restored by Lady Anne Clifford in 1650–60, has an unusual, circular chapel 30ft (9m) in diameter.

Beckermonds   A tiny hamlet in upper Wharfedale where Oughtershaw and Greenfield Becks unite to become the River Wharfe, which then enjoys a couple of miles of free, joyous, frolicsome youth with roadside access all the way. Above Beckermonds a narrow, winding road ventures over the watershed to Hawes; another heads westwards only so far as High Greenfield, engulfed by conifer plantations that darken the once bare hillsides of Langstrothdale.

*Bishopdale   Wensleydale's main tributary valley, a mile wide at its northern end between West Burton and Thoralby, but narrowing to its south-west where Kidstones Pass carries the B6160 over the watershed to Wharfedale. Silt from a glacial lake has given it a rich soil. In medieval times it was a hunting forest in the Honour of Middleham, but in the seventeenth century became the home of prosperous yeomen who built splendid farmhouses.

Blea Moor   Appropriately named bleak moorland between Ribble Head and Dent Head penetrated by the famous, or infamous, Blea Moor Tunnel of the Settle–Carlisle line, its course identified by a line of air-shafts.

*Bolton Abbey   A misnomer resulting from long usage for the small Wharfedale village which developed near the entrance to Bolton Priory, whose hauntingly beautiful ruins grace an exquisite, tranquil riverside setting. Romillys, Cliffords and Percys in medieval times, and the Earls of Burlington and Dukes of Devonshire since 1748, have developed the Wharfedale estates to their present wooded parkland, as attractive to today's visitors as it was inspiring to Girtin, Turner and Landseer. Nothing but harmony in a man-made landscape.

Bordley   No motor road reaches this remote hamlet between Grassington and Malham, at the heart of Fountains Abbey's vast estates on Malham Moor. Walkers can appreciate the solitudes of surrounding pastures. The so-called Stone Circle near the end of Malham Moor Lane is probably the remains of a Bronze Age burial mound.

*Braithwaite Hall   This 1667 house, now a working farm, faces north across lower Wensleydale between East Witton and Coverham. National Trust property since 1941, it can be visited by prior arrangement with the tenants.

Brigflatts   A former flax-weavers' hamlet in the Rawthey valley below Sedbergh. Its Friends' meeting-house of 1675, one of the earliest in the North of England, with mullioned windows and a gallery round three sides, is a cool, tranquil haven of peace and learning. In spring's fullness its setting is idyllic.

Buckden   Settled as a forest village serving Langstrothdale, the old name given to upper Wharfedale. A few scattered houses round a green, surrounded by majestic scenery, with good walks and climbs abounding, including Buckden Pike, 2,302ft (702m).

*Burnsall   A Domesday village where Wharfedale's landscape changes. Below, the valley is well wooded, and moors and walls are sombre, dark with gritstone; above is limestone country of green pastures, gleaming scars and white walls. St Wilfred's church has unusual lychgate, Anglo-Danish crosses, Norse hogback tombstones. Next door is the former grammar school of 1602, and the village street has many neat houses. Carpark near the handsome bridge encourages exploration of riverside paths.

Burtersett   Wensleydale village near Hawes with many cottages built last century for quarrymen who worked in underground stone mines whose spoil-heaps on the hillsides above are memorials to an industry which flourished between 1860 and 1930.

Buttertubs   Vertical shafts near the crest of the pass between Hawes and Thwaite are the most easily seen potholes in the Dales, formed only by the eroding action of water. The deepest, about 60ft (18m) are on the east side of the road; can be approached closely, with care. Surrounding landscape wild and majestic, with magnificent views down into Swaledale.

Calf, The   At 2,220ft (677m) the highest of a score of rounded grassy summits on the Howgill Fells, reached by a short, steep climb from Cautley (q.v.) or a longer, gentler climb from Sedbergh via Winder and Calders. The National Park boundary crosses The Calf on its east–west alignment between the Rawthey and Lune valleys.

Cam   Cam Fell forms the watershed between Langstrothdale and Gayle Beck in upper Ribblesdale. The Pennine Way follows the course of a Roman road along its crest from Cam End to Kidhow Gate, just over 2 miles.

Carlton   Main village in Coverdale, with long street and eighteenth-century houses, and good views across valley to Flamstone Pin and Roova Crags.

Carperby   Linear village of Danish settlement on north side of Wensleydale. Well-kept green has market-cross of 1674, attractive houses and farms, and a Classical-style Friends' meeting-house of 1864. Nearby hillsides show good examples of lynchets (see Chapter 3) and, to the north-west, piles of quarried flagstones stand near cave-like entrance of the Carperby stone mine, worked last century. To south of road, pleasant field path leads to Freeholders' Wood and Aysgarth Falls.

*Castle Bolton   Village on Wensleydale's northern hillside dominated by massive fourteenth-century castle with four corner towers and four domestic ranges between, now a restaurant and museum. Mary Queen of Scots imprisoned here, in great comfort, July 1568 to January 1569. Village is worth more than a second glance, with two-row lay-out and green between. St Oswald's church used as exhibition centre during summer months. Convenient carpark has panoramic views across the dale.

Cautley   In Rawthey valley 4 miles north-east of Sedbergh along A683. The east-facing Cautley Crags is the best rock outcrop in the Howgills, and Cautley Spout a fine 700ft (213m) cascade, reached by a footpath from the Cross Keys Inn, built 1600, altered in eighteenth and nineteenth centuries, now a Temperance Hotel owned by National Trust.

*CB   Hamlet and hotel in Arkengarthdale, named after seventeenth-century lord of the manor, Charles Bathurst. Lead-mining associations all round, with octagonal powder-house c1800 a neat, unique focus. Wild roads lead north to Teesdale, west to Tan Hill, south to Swaledale.

*Chapel-le-Dale   Hamlet and inn on B6255 4 miles north-east of Ingleton. Accident victims of construction of Settle–Carlisle railway commemorated in the tiny church. Caves and potholes abound, but Ingleborough commands the scene and tempts the limbs. Route crosses superb limestone pavement at Souther Scales (nature reserve). Across the valley, Whernside is a sterner climb.

*Clapham   The A65 between Settle and Ingleton bypasses this charming village which has three claims to fame: Michael Faraday, pioneer of electricity, was local blacksmith's son; Reginald Farrer, exploring plant-hunter who introduced many Eastern plants to Britain, lived at manor; famous monthly magazine *Yorkshire Dalesman* (now *Dalesman*) begun here 1939 and still published in village. Beck flows down centre of village between two roads; many bridges and trees. Very good centre for limestone walks to north. National Park Centre and carpark.

Clough, River   Garsdale's river flows westwards to join the Rawthey near Sedbergh, and below Danny Bridge its gorge forms the main feature of the Sedgwick geology trail.

*Colt Park Wood   Nature reserve of ash woodland on limestone pavement near Ribble Head, on north-eastern flanks of Ingleborough. Access by permit only.

*Conistone   Delightful little village of limestone houses and farms on east side of Wharfedale, opposite Kilnsey Crag. Riverside pastures, former arable fields on hillside strip lynchets, and common pasture on fells. Conistone Dib concentrates the limestone ethos into a splendid dry valley gorge behind the village.

Cotterdale   One of Wensleydale's 'little dales' above Hawes, with a farm and a handful of cottages by the beck. Old coalpits pockmark the slopes of Shunner Fell, but an earlier wildness is now smoothed beneath conifers. Cotter Force, near the main road, is worth the short walk.

Coverdale   Wensleydale's most easterly tributary valley opens out between Middleham and East Witton. The narrow road up the dale meets wild country in its upper reaches, and crosses the watershed into Wharfedale. Formerly part of the Honour of Middleham it once had one of the early main roads into the Dales, from London, via Barnsley and Skipton. Caldbergh and West Scrafton are small villages on the east side of the lower dale, Melmerby on the west, with a road over the moor to West Witton. Coverdale was the birthplace in 1488 of Miles Coverdale who first translated the Bible into English.

*Coverham Abbey   Two miles south-west of Middleham, but only scanty remains of the 1212 foundation built by White Canons of the Premonstratensian Order, most stones having been incorporated into the adjoining farm and its buildings. Two fourteenth-century arches, an ornate window, and part of gatehouse survive. Visible from public footpath.

Craven Old Way   Old pack-horse track and drove road between Dent and Ingleton, crossing Whernside's northern shoulder. Excellent walking, with panoramic views, spaciousness, skylark song and sheep.

*Crummackdale   Rock-strewn valley north of Austwick, for walkers rather than motorists. Valley head is a wilderness of clints, boulders, scars and pavements, lonely and lovely at Beggar's Stile and Thieves' Moss, and the pack-horse tracks to Selside and Horton.

Dales Way   Official long-distance footpath from Ilkley to Bowness-on-Windermere. Eighty-one miles following riverside tracks up Wharfedale, high moorland across Cam Fell to Gearstones, then into Dentdale, the lower Rawthey valley, Lune gorge, Kendal and Windermere. Any section is a joy; the whole is memorable, scenically more rewarding and physically less demanding than the Pennine Way.

Dee, River   Dentdale's river, flirtatious and frolicsome in youth, with occasional instincts to vanish beneath its limestone bed. Trees and pastures grace its later course below Dent, blessed by farms and bridges, embraced by hills, to its meeting with the Rawthey below Sedbergh.

Deepdale   Aptly named steep-sided valley with scattered farms on the south side of Dentdale. A minor road climbs the valley head 1 mile west of Whernside's summit, southwards to Kingsdale and Ingleton.

*Dent   Small, compact, intimate village with narrow, winding cobbled streets, whitewashed houses, a large, low-profiled church, a rough-hewn hunk of pink granite commemorating the great Adam Sedgwick, a large carpark with a superb view of Dentdale, and inviting field walks around.

*Dentdale   Clean lines of soaring, tawny fells embrace a broad pastoral valley of dispersed farms. Hedged fields and hedgerow trees create a softer landscape, whose many seventeenth- and eighteenth-century houses deserve to be sought out. Narrow winding roads thread the valley, with main outlet towards Sedbergh. The best view is from Dent station, at 1,150ft (350m) the highest main-line station in Britain. Beyond it, an airy road leads over to Garsdale Head.

*Easby Abbey   A mile from Richmond and just outside the Park boundary.

Reached by road or charming riverside walk. Extensive thirteenth- and fourteenth-century remains of domestic buildings and gate-house; very little of monastic church.

*East Witton   For travellers coming up Wensleydale, the first village within the National Park, 4 miles south-east of Leyburn, on A6108. Long, rectangular green flanked by neat stone cottages of village rebuilding early last century on house plots identical to those of c1627. The roadside church is contemporary with the 'new' estate village.

Embsay   Village of gritstone houses 2 miles north-east of Skipton. Yachts sail on Embsay Reservoir on the moor's edge above the village, and former station is now headquarters of the Yorkshire Dales Railway Preservation Society. The Society has brought back into use a short length of track of original railway which operated passenger service from Ilkley, with freight continuing until 1969.

Feetham   Swaledale village above Reeth, with a sloping green near the Punch Bowl Hotel grazed by cattle, and a moorland road soaring northwards, by Surrender Bridge and the watersplash, to Arkengarthdale.

Feizor   Charming hamlet off the A65 north-west of Settle, with a few farms and cottages loosely grouped round a tiny green, with pump and trough, and limestone uplands beyond.

*Fountains Fell   Gritstone moorland between Malham Tarn and Penyghent. Once owned by Fountains Abbey, now crossed by Pennine Way which passes close to old coalpits and remains of coke oven near the summit at 2,191ft (668m).

Fremington   Small village near Reeth, more famous for long limestone scar of Fremington Edge which forms high wall along the north-east side of Arkengarthdale. The old Richmond road climbs eastwards from Fremington to follow an upland route to the market town.

Gaping Gill   Three miles north of Clapham, reached only by footpath. The best-known pothole in the Dales, with a vertical drop of 340ft (104m). Local caving clubs operate a winch-borne chair for adventurous members of the public at Spring and August Bank Holidays.

Gargrave   Large village just outside the Park's southern boundary, on A65 west of Skipton. Wide green by river, good seventeenth-century houses, and the Leeds–Liverpool Canal for good measure, so towpaths offer contrasting alternative to Pennine Way which pursues a parkland course to Malham.

*Garsdale   Trough-like valley threaded by A684, extending westwards from important Pennine watershed near the Moorcock Inn to Sedbergh. Names and dispersal of farms are sure indication of Norse settlement. Steep sides and creeping afforestation make it a valley to travel through rather than to explore on foot.

*Gayle   Wensleydale village with far deeper roots than neighbouring Hawes. Close-clustered cottages wash their feet in Duerley Beck, which idles or surges over shallow limestone shelves favoured by geese and ducks. Narrow alleys have whimsical names – Gaits, Beckstones, Marridales, Wynd, Hargill and Thundering Lane. Knitting flourished as a cottage industry, and cotton-mill (1784), still standing, soon turned to spinning woollen yarn for local knit-hosiers. Worked until 1850. Tall houses in Beckstones were combing-houses. Old Hall has ostentatious doorhead of 1695.

*Giggleswick   Across the Ribble from Settle, and only touched by the A65. Has much architectural interest, with good seventeenth-century houses, many having date panels on carved lintels. Noble church, mainly fifteenth century, contains good seventeenth-century woodwork. Explore path by Tems Beck for more cottage groups and observe how village is dominated by the impressive greened copper dome (1901) of Giggleswick School Chapel. To north-west Giggleswick Scar superbly illustrates the scarp formed by the South Craven Fault.

*Gordale Scar Impressive limestone gorge east of Malham probably formed through the collapse of a cave system. Demands a closer look, so walk the field path as far as the ravine entrance, where the wind whistles down between sheer walls of limestone 150ft (45m) high, only 30ft (9m) wide at base. Higher up, a waterfall emerges through a hole, with a tufa screen adjoining. It all terrified the early tourists and artists; we should look with awe at the work of water and weather.

On the opposite side of the road, Janet's Foss and Little Gordale (National Trust) enchant the eye and calm the spirit in a sylvan setting.

*Grassington Wharfedale's most important village has the vitality and character of a small town, and retains a friendly, intimate atmosphere. Important roads crossed here: Skipton–Pateley Bridge, and the road up Wharfedale. Monastic travellers, medieval traders, eighteenth-century lead-miners, textile workers, train-borne tourists in the first thirty years of this century, and more recent car-borne visitors, have all played their part in the Grassington story. Surrounding landscape shows evidence of two thousand years of farming. Splendid situation, and good centre, shops and facilities contribute to increasing popularity and prosperity. Large carpark adjoins National Park office: much to explore locally, but there is no Anglican church – this is across the river at Linton. Grassington hosts a lively arts festival in June and an art exhibition in August.

*Grass Wood Yorkshire Wildlife Trust nature reserve a mile north-west of Grassington. Twenty acres (8ha) of ash-dominant woodland, over limestone cliffs, pavement and consolidated scree. Very rich woodland flora and bird life. Public footpaths from Grassington, and from the Conistone road, give access.

Greenhow Hill Isolated village on Bewerley Moor, a mile outside Park boundary on Grassington–Pateley Bridge road. Its 1,300ft (400m) situation is unenviable. Developed as lead-mining settlement in eighteenth and nineteenth centuries, but many of its remote small houses and walled crofts originated in the seventeenth century, when they were erected on moorland expressly for 'improving the waste . . . and for the keeping of draught oxen and horses for the maintenance of the mines'. Lead-mining ceased about 1880.

Grinton Small Swaledale village of grey stone houses and a grey stone church, for centuries the mother-church of all the valley beyond. The Arkle Beck, coming down Arkengarthdale, joins the Swale at Grinton. Above the village, landscapes are austerely beautiful; below, the maturing valley is softened by woodlands. A narrow road to the west, along Harkerside, passes near the hill fort of Maiden Castle. Roads southwards to Leyburn or Castle Bolton cross splendid heather moors intersected by remote little valleys sad with lead-mining remains.

Grisdale Norse settlers kept pigs here, but now the remote, secret little dale north-west of Garsdale Head is almost empty. Names of lonely farms add their euphony to breezes and birdcall: Round Ing, High Flust, Flust, Fea Fow, and Rowantree at the end of the road. Baugh Fell and Swarth Fell brood over a deserted land.

*Gunnerside   The road from Reeth up Swaledale crosses from north to south, after passing through the huddle of houses. Walls stitch the fields and fells in crazy patterns, knotted by scores of barns. A path leads up east side of Gunnerside Gill by the laughing beck. After a mile of woods and pastures it emerges into the majestic grandeur of a wild upland valley dramatised by memories and remains of centuries of lead-mining. One for the connoisseur of landscapes of toil and endeavour.

Halton Gill   Best to come across it suddenly, from the south, by the upland road from Stainforth, in Ribblesdale, along Penyghent's eastern flanks. The descent into the head of Littondale delights the eye, especially in late spring. Halton Gill's handful of houses and farms have date panels showing seventeenth-century origins. Their grouping round a small green with trees is memorably evocative, and the road down Littondale needs only to be sauntered.

*Hardraw Force   Famous spout-like waterfall, 1¼ miles north of Hawes, plunges 90ft (27m) over Yoredale strata, in a natural amphitheatre setting with such good acoustics that band concerts are sometimes held there. Tourist attraction since early last century. Access (small charge) through Green Dragon in Hardraw village.

*Hawes   Small market town in upper Wensleydale, 850ft (260m) above sea-level, surrounded by sweeping fells. Market charter granted as recently as 1700. Situation makes it ideal as a market and tourist centre, with A684 passing through the town, and upland roads linking it to Kirkby Stephen, Swaledale, Wharfedale and Ribblesdale. Has good range of shops, hotels, guest-houses, holiday cottages, camp and caravan sites, and youth hostel. Large carpark by National Park Information Centre in old station yard. Nearby Upper Dales folk museum, based on excellent local history and 'folk' collections developed by Marie Hartley and Joan Ingilby, is a 'must', as should be the Hawes Ropeworks. Auction Mart has a huge through-put of livestock, and open-air market always fascinating. (Market day: Tuesday.)

Hawkswick   Attractive riverside hamlet in lower Littondale, with houses and barns of limestone, beneath brackeny slopes and limestone scars. Some interesting modern conversions.

Healaugh   Small Swaledale village above Reeth, evolved in the twelfth century on the edge of forest waste.

Hebden   East of Grassington on the Pateley Bridge road. Gritstone houses and cottages flank the west side of Hebden Beck, whose upper valley was on the edge of the vast lead-mining area of Grassington and Hebden Moors. Miles of inviting paths all round.

Hell Gill   Nowhere is the National Park boundary, or that between North Yorkshire and Cumbria, as wild and fierce as this, on the western slopes of Lunds Fell near the source of the River Ure. A footpath reaches it from Aisgill Moor Cottages; a windy, high-level former drove road from Kirkby Stephen to Hawes crosses it at Hell Gill Bridge, a single arch spanning a deep, dark, awesome limestone gorge fully meriting its name.

Helwith Bridge   Ancient east–west crossing of the River Ribble 4 miles north of Settle. Quarries scar Moughton's hillsides, once providing massive slates for paving-slabs, roofs, shelves, the sides of rainwater tanks, and tombstones. Now, with the nearby limestone, it is merely used for road metal. Interesting road leads westwards to Wharfe and Austwick.

Hetton   Linear village in southern part of Park, north of Skipton. Bridlepaths lead northwards to Boss Moor, Bordley, Hetton Common and Winterburn Reservoir. The minor road westwards crosses pleasant landscapes to Malham.

*Horton-in-Ribblesdale   Midway between Settle and Ribble Head, village is ideally situated for exploring Ribblesdale's limestone landscapes, for climbing Penyghent and/or Ingleborough, or for sampling the Pennine Way. Useful carpark, pub, cafes, interesting church. Only the huge quarries jar the eye; man-made limestone scars depress – natural ones enrich.

*Howgill Fells   Forty square miles of green, smooth-sided, lonely fells, open grassland above lower intake walls. Rivers Rawthey and Lune almost encircle the hills, where long, lonely valleys penetrating the northern sector are quiet paradises for discerning walkers. Easiest access, however, from Sedbergh, Cautley and Howgill Lane.

*Hubberholme   Church, inn and a couple of farms, yet for many this is Wharfedale's special gem. St Michael and All Angels is a place of pilgrimage, in idyllic riverside setting, with profile echoing background hills. Memorable interior. George Inn has thousand-year-old 'Poor Pasture' letting ceremony, when local farmers bid for tenancy of 16 acre (6ha) field. Hubberholme bridge was important crossing on old trade route between Lancaster and Newcastle.

Hull Pot   Large, cavernous pothole near Pennine Way, 2 miles north of Horton-in-Ribblesdale. No need to descend to appreciate its size and structure.

*Ingleborough   Best-known and loved of the 'Three Peaks', familiar to thousands of climbers, its 2,372ft (723m) summit cairn on a broad plateau. Impressive from any direction, its stepped profile, on vast limestone platform, lifts the spirit and kindles curiosity about the nature of this lovely rock. Climbable from any direction, most easily from Ingleton via Fell Lane and Crina Bottom, most directly from Chapel-le-Dale. Panoramic views from summit.

Ingleborough Cave   Show cave, 1½ miles walk from Clapham through Clapdale Woods. First opened in 1837, now lit by electricity, with many formations to be seen along its 600yd (550m) passage.

*Ingleton   Just outside the Park's southern boundary, a small, busy market town developed as a tourist centre in early Victorian times. Narrow winding streets, old mills, and terraces of cottages in shadow of former railway viaduct. 'The Falls Walk' (small charge) originated as an attraction in 1884, along wooded valleys of Rivers Doe and Twiss, and continues its appeal. Amid such natural beauty it is hard to associate Ingleton with the coal-mining of early this century. Unsightly developments on edges of Ingleton are unfortunate blemishes.

*Keld   Small is beautiful in this last village along the road up Swaledale. A few houses, cottages, and a couple of chapels cluster round a tiny square above the river rushing through its wooded gorge. Farms and barns dot the embracing hills. Pennine Way walkers converge on the youth hostel, others savour the peaceful timelessness. Roads lead beyond to the wild solitude of the upper dale and the temptations of Tan Hill. Abundance of waterfalls.

*Kettlewell   Capital of upper Wharfedale in a superb setting. Large village of textile and lead-mining memories, with most of its houses and cottages tucked away from the main valley road crossing two bridges, with riverside carpark between. Miles of paths and green lanes invite exploration, along the river and on the limestone hills.

Kidstones Pass The main route between Wharfedale and Wensleydale reaches 1,390ft (424m) above Buckden. Immediately south of this the road follows a short stretch of Roman road (Kidstones Causeway) which crosses the Stake pass. Fine views of Wharfedale and Bishopdale.

*Kilnsey Formidably thrusting Kilnsey Crag dominates a handful of houses by the Wharfedale road. Behind the popular Tennant Arms, Old Hall (1648) occupies site of famous monastic grange. Nearby, Kilnsey Park Visitor Centre concentrates on freshwater fish, offering trout-fishing lakes and a feeding pond. Farm shop stocks fresh fish, game and poultry. Riverlife Museum includes audio-visual displays. Kilnsey Show (Tuesday after August Bank Holiday Monday) is big annual event in Dales calendar.

Kisdon 'Island' hill, 1,636ft (499m) in upper Swaledale. River flows along north and east sides, road between Muker and Keld keeps to south and west, above the Swale's pre-Ice Age course. Corpse Way crosses Kisdon, Pennine Way contours it high above the valley.

Langcliffe One mile north of Settle, but missed by the main valley road. Spacious green with informal cottage terraces around. Cotton-spinning community from late eighteenth century; mill now manufactures paper. Road to Malham climbs steeply out of village, provides excellent viewpoints for Ribblesdale and sweeping fells.

*Langstrothdale The old forest name given to upper Wharfedale above Buckden. Its new forest beyond Beckermonds is, however, coniferous.

*Langthwaite Main community in Arkengarthdale. Former lead-miners' cottages are clenched round a tiny square by Arkle Beck, beneath wooded hill. To west, parish church is a 'Commissioners' church', built after Waterloo with funds

Walling competition at Kilnsey Show

largely provided by Parliament – the only Dales example. Interesting, if not particularly appealing.

*Leyburn   Wensleydale's chief market town, just outside the Park boundary. Late Georgian buildings round two market places endow the town with feeling of spacious prosperity enlivened on market days (Fridays). Popular tourist centre with good amenities and wide view to Wensleydale's fields and distant hills.

*Ling Gill   National Nature Reserve in upper Ribblesdale, a gill wood of 12 acres (5ha) in limestone gorge, with important tree and plant life. Can be seen from Pennine Way 4 miles north of Horton. No permit required for visiting.

*Linton   Beautiful Wharfedale village off B6160 a mile south-west of Grassington. Wealth of seventeenth- and eighteenth-century buildings round large green, with variety of bridges crossing Linton Beck. Fountaine Hospital architecturally significant. Important industrial hamlet near river, on road to Linton church, which serves four townships. Field and riverside paths lead to charming corners.

*Littondale   Valley of the River Skirfare, joining Wharfedale above Kilnsey; takes its name from Litton, near valley head, a small linear village of neat limestone cottages, houses and barns. Charles Kingsley called the valley 'Vendale', Wordsworth named it 'Amerdale' and ITV selected it originally as the setting for the 'Emmerdale Farm' series. Bare limestone etches hillsides unscarred by industry; riverside paths are tempting, valley roads winding, reaching crescendos of upland landscapes, to Stainforth or Malham.

Low Row   Unpretentious Swaledale village between Reeth and Gunnerside, which merges into Feetham. Minor road crosses river to Crackpot and Summer Lodge.

Maiden Castle   Defensive earthwork, probably of Romano–British date, on south side of Swaledale west of Grinton. In heather and bracken just above minor road, covers about 2 acres (0.8ha), with good rampart and ditch surrounding it. Hundred-yard avenue of parallel stones to east.

*Malham   Outstandingly important village at heart of Craven country, 5 miles north of A65 at Gargrave. Natural stagecraft has given it a superb situation below scarp of the Mid Craven Fault. Long history of settlement on limestone uplands; sheep-farming on monastic estates paved way for later prosperity; splendid farms and barns, and miles of gleaming limestone walls, yield dominance to natural wonders of Malham Cove, pavement, gorges, dry valleys and vanishing waters. Mighty, magical landscapes of Britain's finest limestone scenery, yet field paths lead to places of intimate charm. National Park Centre and large carpark, but summer weekend hordes swamp the sensitivity.

Mallerstang   Important north–south valley of upper course of River Eden, outside National Park, traversed by road from Hawes to Kirkby Stephen, and Settle–Carlisle railway. Pendragon Castle (ruin) formerly a home of the Cliffords.

Marrick   Hill-top village in Swaledale, below Reeth. Meagre ruins of twelfth-century priory near river separated from village by stone-causeway, the 'Nuns' Steps'. Important eighteenth- and nineteenth-century lead-mining and smelting east of village.

Marske   Village in lower Swaledale. Idyllic setting on north side of valley by Marske Beck, with wooded hills around. Good walks by Marske Beck to Orgate, Telfit and Helwith – former lead-mining area. Fine upland walk eastwards to

Linton, Wharfedale. The packhorse bridge was originally probably sixteenth century and was repaired in the late seventeenth century by Elizabeth Redmayne. Note the ford alongside the bridge

Applegarth and Richmond, but motorists may prefer the high-level 'old' road.

*Mastiles Lane The most famous 'green road' in the Dales, crossing Malham Moor between Malham and Kilnsey. Busy monastic route, now its airy undulations and quiet are enjoyed by walkers, riders and cyclists.

*Middleham Village in lower Wensleydale with character and historic importance of small market town. Massive castle of the proud Nevilles and their successors; briefly a royal home. Three-storey Georgian house and inns front two market places. Church was formerly collegiate, and author Charles Kingsley one of its honorary canons. Two centuries of racehorse training at Middleham continue today, with about two hundred horses under eight or nine trainers. Expect strings of them exercising on local roads or galloping over open common land on Low Moor.

*Muker Houses of grey-brown stone above Muker Beck in upper Swaledale, with river valley beyond and a background of majestic hills. Every prospect pleases, and every walk delights. Since 1974 Muker has been the home of Swaledale Woollens Ltd, a small company selling garments knitted in the area by outworkers in their homes.

*Nappa Hall Fortified house (1460) on north side of Wensleydale east of Askrigg. Partially visible from road, better appreciated from footpath to its west.

Newby Small village with green, off A65 between Ingleton and Clapham. Newby Hall occupies site of former grange of Furness Abbey.

Nidderdale Wholly and inexcusably excluded from the National Park. Above Pateley Bridge, much of valley and its surrounding moors is orientated to provid-

Middleham market place

ing Bradford's water, but the reservoirs of Gouthwaite (1901), Angram (1919) and Scar House (1936) impart a distinctive character to the dale. Before then, Nidderdale was industrialised, with lead-mining and smelting, and the growth of flax for linen and hemp. Ramsgill is the prettiest village, Middlesmoor the most spectacularly situated, while from Lofthouse (between them) a useful moorland road crosses the watershed northwards to lower Wensleydale. Geological and scenic features include How Stean, a splendid limestone gorge, near Lofthouse, and Brimham Rocks, near Pateley Bridge, where on 360 acres (145ha) of moorland is the most remarkable group of naturally eroded gritstone rocks in England, visited by tourists for two hundred years and now a National Trust property. (Car-parking charge).

*Norber Boulders   Site of great geological importance a mile north of Austwick. Sloping limestone plateau littered with huge boulders of dark Silurian slate carried by ice-sheet from a source half a mile away and dumped. Erosion of limestone has left boulders perched on low pedestals.

Oxnop   Moor road from Askrigg to Muker crosses watershed at 1,633ft (498m), descends into Swaledale on west side of Oxnop Gill, sheltered ravine with gill wood, tumbling beck, rich in wild life, a favourite with the Kearton brothers, pioneer local photographic naturalists. Oxnop Scar is a fine limestone exposure and magnificent viewpoint.

Parcevall Hall   Much altered seventeenth-century house near Appletreewick in Wharfedale; now a diocesan retreat. Beautiful gardens open daily between Easter and October.

Pen Hill   Wensleydale's most famous hill, 1,725ft (526m) high. Ancient beacon site, easily climbed from crest of moor road between West Witton and Melmerby. Displays craggy face to north, overlooking dale and vast, dreary peat moor to the south, flanked by Bishopdale and Coverdale.

*Penyghent   At 2,273ft (694m), the lowest (sic) of the Three Peaks, but the easiest to climb; the shortest route up the stepped, southern 'nose' which is from

Dale Head, 3 miles north-east of Stainforth, and involves some scrambling. The Pennine Way uses this approach, descending via Hull Pot to Horton. Westwards is the Ribblesdale landscape, with Ingleborough across the valley; eastwards is Littondale, with Malham to the south-east. Choose a bright, breezy day for the best rewards, and, by the western crags, look for the finger-like pinnacle. In summer, mountain saxifrage makes the steep rock face purple with its delicate flowers.

Raven Seat   Swaledale's most remote hamlet, where Whitsundale Beck froths down a lonely, secret valley 3 miles above Keld. Only two houses are now occupied, but in early eighteenth century seven families were enough to support a chapel and a pub. Surviving pack-horse bridge indicates earlier importance.

Rawthey, River   Begins on Baugh Fell, flows north-westwards down Uldale, then south-west to Sedbergh along the south-eastern corner of the Howgill Fells. Joins River Lune below Middleton Bridge on the A683 Sedbergh–Kirkby Lonsdale road.

Raydale   A short, wide valley south of Semerwater, fed by Bardale Beck, Raydale Beck and Cragdale Water draining northwards from the Wensleydale–Wharfedale watershed. Bardale and Cragdale are wild and lovely, but a dark blanket of conifers now clothes Raydale's once sheepy fellside. Some may even call this environmental gain.

Redmire   Wensleydale village just outside National Park boundary, on north side of valley. Main axis, unusually, lies north–south; good seventeenth- and eighteenth-century houses, and some less satisfactory modern ones, round an irregular, tree-graced green. Quiet lane leads to isolated church, dignified and simple, with Norman doorway. Pleasant field, wood and parkland path to Wensley. Coal- and lead-miners worked moorland pits to north during last two centuries.

*Reeth   Twelve miles west of Richmond, Swaledale divides, the main valley continuing west to Keld, with Arkengarthdale branching north-westwards. Reeth commands the junction from its superb site 600ft (180m) up on Calva's eastern spur. Important market centre in eighteenth and nineteenth centuries, when lead-mining and domestic hand-knitting thrived. Elegant Georgian houses and inns face across large, sloping triangular green with wide views. Very good centre for local exploration and excellent walks. Former Methodist schoolroom now houses Swaledale Folk Museum where the exhibits illuminate much local history. Seven fairs and a Friday market now reduced to important show in early September and lively autumn sheep sales.

*Ribble Head   The Three Peaks look down on this vast, elevated, moorland hollow, at 1,000ft (305m). Enormous railway viaduct of 1876 strides across wild landscape of wind-blown bent and limestone scars. Here, the Ribblesdale road, B6479, branches from the B6255, Hawes–Ingleton road, and a large triangle of grass below the Station Inn provides carparking space and a base for climbers seeking the fells and potholers preferring the depths. Ordinary mortals merely enjoy the frolicsome river, the fascination of friendly limestone scars, and the splendid spaciousness.

*Ribblesdale   Ten mile valley between Ribble Head and Settle, flanked by Ingleborough and Penyghent. Glaciation gave the upper valley its rounded hummocks (called drumlins) and created difficulties for farmers and the makers of roads and railway. A succession of tracks along and across the valley imprint their two thousand years of use. Green lanes lead to Wensleydale, Wharfedale and

Crummackdale. Ingman Lodge is the most impressive of the scattered farms. Below Settle Ribblesdale becomes calmer and more sylvan in its maturity.

*Richmond   Hill-top situation above River Swale gives visual excitement; Norman castle provides deep roots and a focal dominance. Cobbled market place, radiating narrow streets, variety of buildings contribute to unique character and 'sense of place', which, the castle apart, is essentially Georgian, exemplified in Newbiggin and Frenchgate. Climb the castle keep for a jackdaw's-eye view of the town and its surroundings; enjoy Castle Walk for dramatic river scenery, and explore the 'wynds' for surprises, including Royal Georgian Theatre of 1788. Like good food, Richmond should be savoured slowly.

Rylstone   Village on the main road between Skipton and Grassington, with a few houses round a pond – a Dales rarity – and others hidden from the road.

*Sedbergh   Western gateway to the Dales only 5 miles from M6 (junction 37) and a good centre for exploring Dentdale, Garsdale, Rawthey valley and Howgill Fells. Market charter dates from 1251, market day, Wednesday. Domestic knitting industry based on local farms flourished from seventeenth to early nineteenth century. Small cotton-mills developed at Birks, Howgill and Millthrop, and a woollen-mill at Hebblethwaite Hall. Town's yards had workshops, stables and spinning-galleries. Chantry school founded 1525, becoming free grammar school 1552, rebuilt 1716 and made public school 1874. Buildings and playing-fields along Sedbergh's southern edge. Town has strong Quaker links. Good walks by rivers and on Howgill Fells.

Selside   Hamlet in upper Ribblesdale, with good seventeenth- and eighteenth-century farmhouses.

*Semerwater   On Wensleydale's southern side, reached by twin roads from Bainbridge, the largest natural lake in the Dales is half a mile long, but almost 2 miles round and quite shallow. Accessible only at its northern shore, near outlet of River Bain, it attracts summer crowds of picnickers, anglers, canoeists, windsurfers and yachtsmen but in winter it is left to the wildfowl and the winds. Fine view of lake from road above Countersett, village with good seventeenth-century houses and strong Quaker associations. Beyond southern end of Lake, Marsett is a village of working farms around a rough, untidy green, while Stalling Busk, on a hillside shelf to the east, is close-clustered and friendly, at the foot of the road crossing the Stake pass. An unusual ruined but partially restored church in fields below village.

*Settle   Busy, important market town on A65, between Ribblesdale's upland pastoral farming and the mixed farming of the lower valley. Market square crammed on Tuesdays with colourful stalls displaying wide range of produce, materials and craft goods. Friendly family shops around and good carparking (free) ensure continued popularity. Townscapes are intimate, compact and faithful to past centuries, more so than any other Dales town. Yards, squares, workshops, houses, cottages and inns reflect growth in trade and activity since the Keighley–Kendal turnpike improved communications from 1753. Do not miss The Folly (1675), nor the short, steep challenge of Castleberg, for rewarding views.

Settle–Carlisle Railway   Really the Leeds–Carlisle main LMS line, with the Settle–Kirkby Stephen section the most breathtakingly scenic of any British main line. It took six years to build, opening for passengers in 1876. The famous 'long drag' from Settle, up Ribblesdale, across Ribble Head, Dent Head, Arten Gill, and Dandry Mire Viaducts, through Blea Moor and Rise Hill Tunnels, takes the line from just under 500ft (152m) to the Aisgill summit at 1,169ft (356m) in 20 miles. A few freight trains and fewer passenger trains now use the line, whose future is in doubt. However, 'Dales Rail' specials from Leeds or Bradford to Carlisle, or Carlisle southwards, on occasional summer weekends, for walkers heading for the Dales and Dales folk going city-shopping. In 1985, 4,800 passengers were carried on these special services which are arranged through the National Park offices.

Shunner Fell   2,348ft (716m) mountain at the head of Swaledale crossed by south–north section of Pennine Way between Hardraw in Wensleydale and Thwaite in Swaledale. Motorists glimpse its dark heather and peat-hags to the west of the Buttertubs Pass.

*Skipton   Southern gateway to the Dales, and largest market town in area. Major trunk roads meet here and, to the north, Wharfedale and Craven beckon. Busy, bustling and lively, with a Clifford castle, a proud church at the top of crowded High Street, the terminal Springs branch of the Leeds–Liverpool Canal, factories, multiple stores and wonderful landscapes within a few minutes' drive.

Stainforth   Compact village on east side of Ribblesdale, centred on small green by Cowside Beck. Nearby, Stainforth Bridge (1670) (National Trust) spans the Ribble in a charming wooded valley where the river falls over limestone ledges into a large pool. Moorland road to east, many old tracks around.

Stang, The   Wild moorland road from CB in Arkengarthdale northwards over the watershed at 1,676ft (511m) and out of the National Park into Teesdale at Barnard Castle.

Starbotton   Upper Wharfedale village of attractive houses and barns, mainly of limestone. Riverside walks and upland pack-horse tracks.

Strid, The   Between Bolton Abbey and Barden, the River Wharfe is squeezed into a narrow rock channel through which it surges with fearsome force. Very dramatic and potentially dangerous. Nature trail in nearby woodland is gentler.

Stump Cross   A mile within the National Park boundary on the Grassington–Pateley Bridge road. Discovered accidentally by lead-miners in 1858. Extensive cave system, with only the show cave open to public. Imaginative lighting shows wonderful stalactite and stalagmite formations. Excellent interpretative centre and café.

*Swaledale   Most northerly and austerely beautiful of the main dales, extending 30 miles from the river's source among the Pennine peat-hags on Birkdale Common to Richmond. Except for the upland wilderness, man has created much of the landscape character, from the woodlands of the lower valley to the villages, farms, walls, barns, fields and tracks of the dale beyond Reeth, overlaid by the theme of man's exploitation of the hills for yield of lead. Black-faced Swaledale sheep make their own contribution to the atmosphere of the place.

Swinnergill   Below Keld the East Grain Beck plunges down a mile-long limestone ravine and joins the Swale by Beldi smelt-mill. Guarded by ruins of eighteenth-century Crackpot Hall (farm), heavy with lead-mining memories, it has a secret cave behind a waterfall near the head of the gill, used as a meeting place by Dissenters in days of seventeenth-century religious persecution. If water-level is low, the gorge walk up Swinnergill at beck level is an exciting adventure. The usual track, by Crackpot, continuing eastwards to Gunnerside Gill, is part of the Coast-to-Coast long-distance footpath.

*Tan Hill   Britain's highest pub, at 1,732ft (528m) above sea level, just over the Durham side of the county boundary. Roads from Keld, Arkengarthdale and Brough meet here, and the Pennine Way passes by. A lonely place enjoying 'one far, fierce hour and sweet' on the last Thursday each May, when the annual show of the Swaledale Sheep Breeders' Association takes place. Environment of rocks, heather, wind-blown grass and pub is wholly appropriate for an occasion almost exclusively for local farmers and sheep, and memorable by any standards.

*Thoralby   Scattered village on north side of Bishopdale, with small green and good examples of Dales vernacular building, especially towards Town Head.

*Thornton Force   At the head of the 'Falls Walk' at Ingleton and an important geological site, with the River Twiss tumbling over limestone and up-ended slates into a charming pool. Noble limestone scenery around.

Thornton Rust   Linear village with stone cottages along opposite sides of narrow green, on south side of Wensleydale between Aysgarth and Bainbridge. Interesting field patterns and good example of a scar wood nearby.

Thorpe   Off-the-road village near Burnsall, in 'reef knoll' landscape on south side of Wharfedale. Very impressive Georgian house, with good barns and mature trees nearby.

Three Peaks   Whernside (2,419ft/737m), Ingleborough (2,372ft/723m) and Penyghent (2,273ft/693m) command the landscape of upper Ribblesdale. Each is individually worthy of day's good climb, with Whernside the longest and most demanding. In sequence they present the greatest Yorkshire challenge to walkers and, regrettably, cyclists. But is it necessary to be competitive?

Threshfield   Wharfedale village across the river from Grassington. Seventeenth-century houses and farms round a tiny triangular green with trees and stocks. Behind Old Hall Inn are fragments of medieval buildings, and Threshfield Free Grammar School (1674) is on the back road between Linton and Grassington. Big quarries at Skythorns, by an inviting lane leading to Malham Moor.

Thwaite   Charismatic close-knit village in upper Swaledale, with a few farms and former lead-miners' cottages. Kearton brothers, pioneer natural-history photographers, born here. Lintel with bird and animal carvings decorates doorway of their birthplace. Pennine Way pauses between Shunner Fell and Kisdon.

Trollers Gill   Limestone gorge with small beck, full of atmosphere and rocky splendour north of Appletreewick. Legendary associations with the mysterious Barguest, a large spectral hound of doubtful pedigree.

Trow Gill   Dry valley in limestone at head of Clapdale, 1½ miles north of Clapham, traversed by path to Gaping Gill and Ingleborough.

Victoria Cave   At northern end of Attermire Scar, north-east of Settle, at height of 1,450ft (442m). Discovered 1838, excavated 1870–78 and 1937. Bones of hyenas, hippopotami, elephants, bears, and giant deer have been identified. Reindeer antlers, ivory tools and flints suggest human occupation about 9000BC.

Walden   Valley of Walden Beck south of West Burton in Wensleydale. Minor roads contour each side, but do not meet; western one reaches Walden Head, below Buckden Pike. Pack-horse tracks cross Carlton Moor eastwards to Coverdale. One of the 'secret' dales.

Watlowes   Famous dry valley above Malham Cove, which once carried the outflow from Malham Tarn to the top of the Cove. Wall down the middle is ancient boundary between Fountains Abbey land (west) and Bolton Priory land (east).

Wensley Largely an estate village round a small green at the entrance to Bolton Hall, Wensleydale. Medieval market importance gave its name to the whole valley. Very good church with important woodwork and memorials. Wensley bridge dates from late fourteenth century – see pointed arches on downstream side – and widened in 1818. East of village is Old Glebe Field, a Yorkshire Wildlife Trust nature reserve.

*Wensleydale Broadest and most pastoral of the main dales. Medieval estates of Jervaulx, Middleham and Bolton embraced most of the valley, but from early seventeenth century farming prosperity based on dairying and sheep resulted in fine houses. The only dale with two roads along its length, two market towns (Leyburn and Hawes) and two National Park Centres (Aysgarth and Hawes). Jervaulx monks are thought to have introduced horse-breeding and cheese-making – the latter became a factory process at Hawes at the end of last century. Good communications with neighbouring dales make Wensleydale an increasingly popular tourist centre for the whole area.

West Burton On south side of Wensleydale, has all ingredients of ideal Dales village – cottages, a spacious green with market cross (but never a market!), waterfall, superb setting and even the scanty remains of a small smelt-mill – but no church. For this, villagers went – and still go – to Aysgarth.

West Witton Linear village on south side of Wensleydale. Its original three-day annual Feast is now reduced to the Saturday nearest 24 August (St Bartholomew's Day), with exciting evening climax, the 'Burning of Bartle'.

*Wharfedale The Wharfe is the most accessible of all Dales rivers. From Bolton Abbey up to Beckermonds the valley road is rarely more than a quarter of a mile from the river and especially close in the upper reaches, while the Dales Way gives even more intimate association. Villages almost wash their feet in the water; limestone dominates the landscape above Burnsall, gritstone woodlands and gracious parkland impart sylvan charm to the lower valley, but always it is lovely.

Whernside Highest of the 'Three Peaks', less distinctive in profile. More gritstone and peat, with a number of tarns on its northern and eastern flanks, about 2,000ft (610m). Below them, limestone shelf of Great Wold has ancient drove road from which is best access to whale-back summit ridge on Cable Rake Top.

White Scar Cave Impressive show cave 1¾ miles north of Ingleton, by B6255. Good lighting emphasises the structure and beauty of many varied rock formations.

*Whitfield Gill Superb example of a gill wood in Wensleydale, near Askrigg. Waterfalls and sequences of exposed strata of Yoredale rocks. Access by footpath from village, or from hamlet of Helm.

Widdale Wide, wild valley south-west of Hawes, threaded by road to Ingleton. Maturing conifer plantations debase the landscape.

Winder Grassy, domed hill above Sedbergh 1,551ft (473m), steep, but easily climbed. Panoramic views over Garsdale, Dentdale and Lune valley, with town below. Should not be missed!

*Yelland's Meadow Roadside hay-meadow east of Muker, Swaledale, a 3 acre (1.2ha) nature reserve (Yorkshire Wildlife Trust), designated because of its rich plant life. Stream bisects it and river flows by northern edge. Farmed traditionally.

Free access, but restrictions in May–June as grass matures to hay.

Yockenthwaite   Norse-settled hamlet in upper Wharfedale forms a memorable group in a riverside setting. Seven hundred yards (640m) north-west on north bank, is the best Bronze Age stone circle in the Dales, 25ft (7.6m) diameter with twenty stones.

Yordas Cave   Near the head of Kingsdale by a small wood, 4 miles north of Ingleton. Once a show cave, now open access. Safe, but muddy after rain. Torch advisable.

BIBLIOGRAPHY

Alderson, J. *Under Wether Fell* Wensleydale Press, 1980 (Local history of Hawes parish and people.)

Barringer, J. C. *The Yorkshire Dales* Dalesman, 1984

Boulton, D. *Adam Sedgwick's Dent* R. G. W. Hollett & Son, Sedburgh, 1984 (Facsimile reprint of a classic of Dales history, first published in two volumes 1868, 1870.)

Brooks, S. D. *A History of Grassington* Dalesman, 1979 (Concise local history.)

Brumhead, D. *Geology Explained in the Yorkshire Dales and on the Yorkshire Coast* David & Charles, 1979 (Excellent studies of particular localities, especially of limestone areas, plus Wensleydale and Swaledale.)

Clough, R. T. *The Lead Smelting Mills of the Yorkshire Dales* Privately published, 1960, reprint 1977 (Classic pioneering study of industrial archaeology, superbly illustrated.)

Fieldhouse, R. and Jennings, B. *A History of Richmond and Swaledale* Phillimore & Co, 1978 (Detailed, well-documented, authoritative local history.)

Hallas, C. S. *The Wensleydale Railway* Dalesman, 1984 (Fascinating story of the development, use, decline of this line, 1840–1964.)

Hartley, M. and Ingilby, J. *The Old Hand Knitters of the Dales* Dalesman, 1951
—*Yorkshire Village* Dent 1953, pbk, 1981
(First-rate local history of Askrigg parish.)
—*The Yorkshire Dales* Dent, 1960
—*Yorkshire Portraits* Dent, 1961
—*Life and Tradition in the Yorkshire Dales* Dent, 1968
—*A Dales Heritage* Dalesman, 1982 (Life Stories from Documents and folk memory relating to Wensleydale and Swaledale.)

Hill, D. *In Turner's Footsteps Through the Hills and Dales of Northern England* Murray, 1984 (A modern artist retraces Turner's journeys in the Dales in 1816, visiting the various viewpoints.)

Hoole, K. *Railways in the Yorkshire Dales* Dalesman, 1975

Houghton, F. W. *Upper Wharfedale* Dalesman, 1980

(Local history with strong botanical flavour.)

Howson, W. *An Illustrated Guide to the Curiosities in the Environs of Malham* 1786

Jennings, B. (ed) *A History of Nidderdale* Nidderdale History Group and Sessions of York, 1983
(Although strictly outside the scope of the present book, this detailed local history refers to many factors which influenced other parts of the area.)

Joy, D. *Settle–Carlisle Railway* Dalesman, 1984

Lousley, J. E. *Wild Flowers of the Chalk and Limestone* Collins, 1950

Manley, G. *Climate and the British Scene* Collins, 1952

Pearsall, W. H. *Mountains and Moorland* Collins, 1958

Pevsner, N. *North Riding* Penguin, 1968

—*West Riding* Penguin, 1968

Pontefract, E. and Hartley, M. *Swaledale* Dent, 1934

—*Wensleydale* Dent, 1936

—*Wharfedale* Dent, 1938
(Each has been reprinted many times. Individually and together they present a delightful picture of life in these dales fifty years ago.)

Raistrick, A. *Old Yorkshire Dales* David & Charles, 1967

—*The Pennine Dales* Eyre & Spottiswode, 1968
(Puts the Yorkshire Dales into its wider context, geographically, geologically, historically and socially.)

—*The West Riding of Yorkshire* Hodder & Stoughton, 1970

—*Malham and Malham Moor* Dalesman, 1971

—*The Pennine Walls* Dalesman, 1973

—*Lead Mining in the Mid-Pennines* Bradford Barton, 1973

—*The Lead Industry of Wensleydale and Swaledale* 2 vol Moorland, 1975

Raistrick, A. and Illingworth, J. *The Face of North-West Yorkshire* Dalesman, 1967

Raistrick, A. and Forder, J. & E. *Open Fell Hidden Dale* F. Peters, 1985
(Stunning black and white photographs evoke the essence of the Dales, and Dr. Raistrick's textual summary is a literary masterpiece encapsulating the ethos of the area.)

Sellers, G. *The Yorkshire Dales: A. Walker's Guide to the National Park* Cicerone Press, 1984

Shoard, Marion *The Theft of the Countryside* Temple Smith, 1980

Speakman, C. *Walking in the Yorkshire Dales* Hale, 1982

—*The Dales Way* Dalesman, 1984

—*A Yorkshire Dales Anthology* Hale, 1981

Stephenson, T. *The Pennine Way* HMSO, 1969

Thompson, M. M. *Mallerstang* J. Whitehead (Appleby), 1965

Wainwright, A. *Pennine Way Companion* Westmorland Gazette, 1968

—*A Coast to Coast Walk* Westmorland Gazette, 1973

—*Walks in Limestone Country* Westmorland Gazette, 1970

—*Walks on the Howgill Fells* Westmorland Gazette, 1972

Waltham, A. C. *Limestone and Caves of North-west England* David & Charles, 1974

Waltham, Tony *Caves, Crags and Gorges* Constable, 1985

Walton, J. *Homesteads of the Yorkshire Dales* Dalesman, 1947, 1979

Wright, G. N. *Roads and Trackways of the Yorkshire Dales* Moorland, 1985

INDEX